# The
# RUSSIAN
# WAY

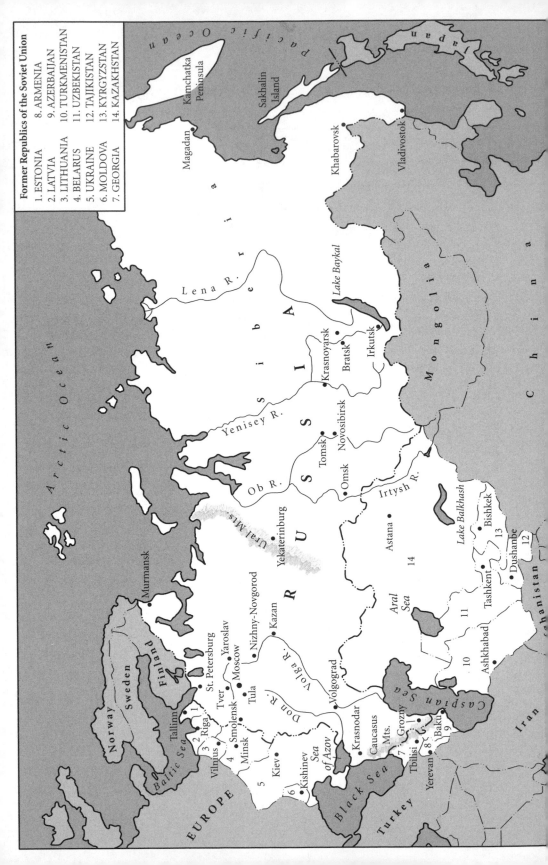

# The RUSSIAN WAY

## Second Edition

*Aspects of Behavior,*

*Attitudes, and Customs*

*of the Russians*

### ZITA DABARS
#### with LILIA VOKHMINA

**McGraw-Hill**

Chicago   New York   San Francisco   Lisbon   London   Madrid   Mexico City
Milan   New Delhi   San Juan   Seoul   Singapore   Sydney   Toronto

**Library of Congress Cataloging-in-Publication Data**

Dabars, Zita D.
    The Russian way : aspects of behavior, attitudes, and customs of the Russians /
Zita Dabars, with Lilia Vokhmina.
        p.   cm.
    Includes index.
    ISBN 0-658-01796-9
    1. Russia (Federation)—Social life and customs.    2. Manners and customs—
Handbooks, manual, etc.    I. Vokhima, L. L. (Lilia Leonidovna).   II. Title.

DK510.762 .D33   2002
306'.0947—dc21                               2001044838

*McGraw-Hill*

*A Division of The McGraw·Hill Companies*

3 4 5 6 7 8 9 0  VRS/VRS  0 9 8 7 6 5

ISBN 0-658-01796-9

This book was set in Minion
Printed and bound by Versa Press

Cover photographs, clockwise from top right: © Emma Lee/Life File/PhotoDisc; © Neil
Beer/PhotoDisc; © David Toase/PhotoDisc; artifact photographs courtesy of the author;
Russian girl photograph courtesy of the author; © C Squared Studios/PhotoDisc

McGraw-Hill books are available at special quantity discounts to use as premiums and sales
promotions, or for use in corporate training programs. For more information, please write to
the Director of Special Sales, Professional Publishing, McGraw-Hill, Two Penn Plaza, New
York, NY 10121-2298. Or contact your local bookstore.

This book is printed on acid-free paper.

# CONTENTS

# CONTENTS

# INTRODUCTION

Every country has its Culture with a "capital C." For Russia, Tchaikovsky, Chekhov, Solzhenitsyn, and icons are representative of its music, literature, and art. Although it is this "Culture" that first comes to mind, every country also has its "small c" culture, which includes the customs and conventions of its people. A knowledge of the habits and practices of the Russian people provides answers to such questions as:

- What items do Russians consider appropriate presents? Why would a young man wooing a Russian girl make the wrong impression by presenting a birthday gift of six yellow roses?
- Why should visitors in a Russian apartment partake sparingly of the cold cuts and salads on the table when they sit down for a meal?
- What does it mean when a black border surrounds one of the names on a list of coauthors in a book?

While in a conversation with an Intourist guide in the former Soviet Union, I took out my calendar to jot down a schedule change. To emphasize what dates the group would be in the country, I had outlined March 16–30 in pen. Upon seeing the calendar, the Intourist guide asked in a hurt voice, "Why would you outline the dates you are in the Soviet Union in black?" I learned then that it is a Russian custom to put a black border around the printed names of people who have died. Of course on future trips, I no longer outlined the dates in black.

Whether the nature of the relationship with a foreign culture is business, professional, or that of a casual tourist, the more sensitivity we have toward the culture's habits, customs, and mores, the greater our satisfaction and pleasure will be.

Scholars who have examined how people react to another culture have found numerous levels of perception. In *Teaching Language in Context* (Boston: Heinle & Heinle, 1993, page 371), Alice Omaggio Hadley presents the levels of cross-cultural awareness developed by Robert Hanley and described by Vicki Galloway at the Northeast Conference on the Teaching of Foreign Languages 1985 Winter Workshop.

Level I: Information about the culture may consist of superficial or visible traits, such as isolated facts or stereotypes. The individual very likely sees the culture as odd, bizarre, and exotic. Ideas are often expressed in terms of what the culture lacks. Culture bearers may be considered rude, ignorant, or unrefined at this stage of understanding.

Level II: Learners at this stage focus on expanded knowledge about the culture in terms of both significant and subtle traits that contrast with those of their own culture. The learners might find the culture bearers' behavior irrational, frustrating, irritating, or nonsensical.

Level III: At this stage, the individual begins to accept the culture at an intellectual level, and thus the culture becomes believable because it can be explained. The individual can see things in terms of the target culture's frame of reference.

Level IV: This level, the level of empathy, is achieved through living in and through the culture. The individual begins to see the culture from the viewpoint of the insider, and thus is able to know how the culture bearer feels.

The aim of *The Russian Way* is to help students, teachers, business travelers, diplomats, and tourists—active or armchair—reach the Level III stage of cultural awareness. Winston Churchill described Russia as "a riddle wrapped in a mystery inside an enigma;" and the nineteenth century

## INTRODUCTION

Russian poet Fyodor Tyutchev wrote: "Russia cannot be understood with the mind . . . One must simply believe in Russia." But there are ways of understanding Russia and the Russians by utilizing knowledge and information about the country. Russians do things in a particular way—a way that may be similar or different from the ways of Americans. Similar or different—not right or wrong. An awareness of these behaviors removes some of the mystery. Just as our appreciation of a painting in a museum is enhanced by knowing something about art, the more knowledge we bring to a culture, the deeper our understanding is of that culture and its people.

The second edition reflects Russian reality at the beginning of the twenty-first century. Where pertinent, the Points of *The Russian Way* have been updated, resulting in significant changes to: "Education," "Politics and Parties," "Restaurants," "Shopping," "Slogans and Statues," and "Telephone." In addition, a few Points have been added to the original ones: "Pensions," "Television and radio," "Tourist Information," and "Zurab K. Tsereteli." The aim of "Tourist Information" is obvious; the other points are there to update the reader on the latest sociological and artistic developments in Russia. Tsereteli was chosen as an artist representative of those who have chosen to stay in Russia and be a part of its artistic vitality. The authors chose "Television and radio" as reflective both of the country's entertainment interests and of a medium that a foreign visitor to Russia, even one who does not know the language, might find accessible.

A note on the translation and transliteration of Russian words in *The Russian Way:* All Russian words and phrases appear in Cyrillic, accompanied by a transliteration into Latin letters and the English translation. In words with two or more syllables, italics in *The Russian Way* the transliteration indicate which syllable is stressed. The transliteration system used is that suggested by J. Thomas Shaw, "The Transliteration of Modern Russian for English-Language Publications," for personal and place names for publications such as newspapers and popular magazines, with the modification that it is being used throughout the book. Soft vowels and palatalized consonants are indicated (i.e., with a "y"), except for the vowel "e" (to avoid words looking like "tyelyevidyeniye" for the Russian word телевидение) and the soft sign. The letter "yeri" is generally transliterated as "i," but on some specific occasions as "y."

# ACKNOWLEDGMENTS

*The Russian Way* manuscript has benefited from suggestions by colleagues and friends in both the United States and the former Soviet Union. In the United States, it was read by Ilya Evstifeev, Melissa Feliciano (Friends School, Baltimore), Steve Frank, Mikhail Gipsov, Olga Hutchins, Aleksandr Jacobson, Taj Johnson, Thora Johnson, Irma Kotok, and George Morris (St. Louis University High School). In Russia, Irina Vorontsova (School #15, Moscow), Emil Vorontsov, and Pyotr Nikolaev (Moscow State University) critiqued portions of the manuscript.

For the second edition, thanks go to Marina Kalinovskaya, Tatyana Kazaritskaya, Olga Eromina, Gregory Ostrov, Ellina Sosenko, Aleksandr Sosenko, Nikita Shcherbakov, Valentina Shcherbakova, Aleksandr Smirnov, Irina Vorontsova, Emil Vorontsov in Moscow and in the United States to Lois Beekey, Ilya Evstifeev, Steve Frank, Olga Hutchins, Stanley Johnson, Betty Lou Leaver, Joseph Liro, Laura McDonald, George Morris, Elizabeth Neatrour, Richard Robin, Kirill Tsivilin, and the members of the SEELANGS Listserv who answered the authors' questions. The authors are also grateful to the American Council of Teachers of Russian and to Middlebury College for sharing the materials they send to Russian-bound students.

Throughout the years, many organizations have enabled me to study, do research, and travel in the former Soviet Union, and grateful thanks is extended to them. The International Research and Educational Exchange (IREX) arranged for teachers to study during summers at Moscow State University. Promoting Enduring Peace sponsored study tours for high school students before it became a common practice to do so. The Geraldine R. Dodge Foundation and the U.S. Department of Education funded parts of the developmental costs of the writing of four-level textbook and video series (starting with *Russian Face to Face*, Level 1 and ending with *Мир русских*), enabling the bilateral team of coauthors to work and live in each other's homes. The Partnership Exchange Program of the American Council of Teachers of Russian (ACTR), funded by the United States Information Agency, allowed my students and me to study and teach at School #15 in Moscow and to live with Russian families. My work at Friends School in Baltimore and at its Center of Russian Language and Culture (CORLAC) has given me the opportunity to present the complexities of Russia to the Friends School community and beyond.

This book is dedicated to the people of Russia: the passerby who took the time to go out of his or her way when I asked for directions, the Intourist guides who were able to convey their love of their country despite the restrictions, and the colleagues and friends who showed me the beauty of their country, the wealth of their culture, and the richness of their history, and who shared with me their professional concerns and invited me into their kitchens.

It was a bleak 2:30 AM when the American author of this book arrived at Sheremetyevo #2 Airport in Moscow to work with colleagues on revising this book and to enjoy the May holidays. Her ride was not to arrive until 7:00 AM. The hours dragged on drearily. At 6:00 the three women behind the counter that serviced arriving flights brewed some tea for themselves—and one woman approached the foreign visitor with a glass of tea. The reviving liquid was as much appreciated as the spontaneous, unsolicited kindness that it represented, typifying Russian generosity.

—Zita Dabars

# 1. ABBREVIATIONS

There are times in a conversation when a nonnative speaker understands a native Russian speaker quite well until something unexpectedly perplexing is said. Often the incomprehensible word turns out to be an abbreviation.

An abbreviation is a shortened form of a word or phrase that is generally, but not always, followed by a period. Some typical English abbreviations are:

| | |
|---|---|
| p. | pint, page |
| AM | ante meridiem |
| sq. yd. | square yard |
| USA | United States of America |

In *The Russian's World* (1974 edition), Genevra Gerhart devotes an entire section (pp. 211–225) to the topic of abbreviations and acronyms in Russian. Her classifications are used in the following section.

## Russian abbreviations, *sokrashcheniya* (*сокраще́ния*)

Russian abbreviations are formed by the first letter of a word, by the first few letters of a word, or by the first letter of each word in a phrase. The abbreviations may be written with or without a period, in small or capital letters.

The following abbreviations are sometimes called *literary* (or conventional) abbreviations "us*lov*nie sokra*shche*niya" (**усло́вные** сокраще́ния), because they are encountered only in written form. (For the pronunciation of Russian letters, see Point 52, "*The Russian Language.*")

| century | в./v. | век/vek |
|---|---|---|
| year | г./g. | год/god |
| women's room | Ж/Zh | Же́нская (убо́рная)/ *Zhen*skaya (u*bor*naya) |
| and so forth | и т.д./i t.d. | и так да́лее/ i tak da*lee |
| deputy, substitute | зам./zam. | замести́тель/ zames*ti*tel |

*Letter* abbreviations, "*buk*vennie sokra*shch*eniya" (бу́квенные сокраще́ния), use the first letter of each word in the names of countries, organizations, factories, and educational institutions. These abbreviations appear in written form and are also used in speech. It is important to know how to pronounce them and whether they should be declined (i.e., inflected depending on the role they play in a sentence).

| Moscow State University | МГУ/MGU [pronounced "em-ge-u"] | Моско́вский госуда́рственный университе́т | Moskovskiy gosu*dars*tvenniy universi*t*et |
|---|---|---|---|
| United States of America | США/SShA [pronounced "se-she-a" or "se-sha"] | Соединённые Шта́ты Аме́рики | Soedin*nyo*nnie *Sht*ati A*m*eriki |
| United Nations | ООН/OON [pronounced "o-on"] | Организа́ция Объединённых На́ций | Organiza*t*siya Obedi*nyo*nnikh *Nat*siy |
| Moscow automobile plant named in honor of Likhachov | ЗИЛ/ZIL [pronounced "zil"] | Заво́д и́мени Лихачёва | Zavo*d* imeni Likha*ch*ova |
| Acquired immune deficiency syndrome (AIDS) | СПИД/SPID [pronounced "speed"] | Синдро́м приобретённого иммунодефици́та | Sind*rom* priob*retyo*nnovo immunodefi*ts*ita |

## Russian syllabic abbreviations

Syllabic abbreviations, "slozhnosokra*shchyo*nnie *slova*"/**сложносо-
кращённые слова́**, are words formed from:

1. The initial syllables of two or more words, e.g.,

| | | |
|---|---|---|
| (school) department head or vice-principal | **за́вуч**/*za*vuch | from **заве́дующий/** *za*veduyushchiy manager, chief **уче́бной ча́ствю/** u*che*bnoy *cha*styu director of students, department head, or vice-principal |

2. The initial syllable of one word plus another whole word, e.g.,

| | | |
|---|---|---|
| nurse | **медсестра́/** medse*stra* | from **медици́нская** medi*tsin*skaya medical, and **сестра́/** se*stra*, sister |
| salary, pay | **зарпла́та/** zar*plata* | from **за́работная пла́та**/za*rabotnaya plat*a, salary |
| office supplies | **канцтова́ры/** kantsto*vari* | from **канцеля́рские това́ры/** kantse*lyar*skie to*vari*, office supplies |

3. The initial syllable of one word plus a *letter* abbreviation, e.g.,

| | | |
|---|---|---|
| city civil registry office | **ГорЗАГС/** Gor*ZAGS* | from **городско́й (отде́л) за́писи а́ктов гражда́нского состоя́ния**/gorod*skoy* (ot*del*) *za*pisi *ak*tov grazh*dan*skovo sosto*yaniya* |

## 2. ADVERTISING

Until 1985, advertising was almost nonexistent in Russia (and in other former Soviet countries) because the economic system was not based on competition. Manufactured goods were produced and distributed on the basis of governmental and party plans, or command economics. Even though "Save Money in Banks" and "Fly Aeroflot" could be seen on the sides of buildings, there was no competition among banks or airline companies because there was only one state bank and one airline company in Russia. To encourage the purchase of insurance, the state insurance company, "Goss*trakh*"/**Госстра́х**, advertised on television. Except for the Pepsi soft drink company, ads for foreign products were nonexistent.

After 1985, individuals were allowed to organize cooperatives in manufacturing and service industries. Small businesses sprang up, markets opened, and local as well as international competition began. As a result, ads started to appear on billboards, in newspapers, and in magazines. For the first time, television and radio programs were interrupted by commercials. Japanese and South Korean companies led the way with advertising for electronic and automotive products. Today Russia is awash with all kinds of ads, including those for cosmetics, cigarettes, beverages of both Russian and foreign production, travel agencies, banks, Internet service providers, cellular phones, business support services, restaurants, and casinos. Two generic ads urge Russians, "Buy Russian-Made Products" and "You Could See Your Ad in This Space."

The trust placed in ads varies. In a *Baltimore Sun* article, "Where Forbidden Is a Possibility," Kathy Lally quotes a Russian woman who states that Russians in the late 1990s still had not gotten over the Soviet-era perception of advertising. "We used to have shortages of anything that was good. [See Point 57, "Shortages and Deficiencies."] They only advertised what they couldn't get rid of. We depended on our friends and neighbors for everything, to tell us what was good and where to buy it. Our tradition is that if something is advertised, it isn't any good."

In the 2000s, advertising in magazines has really taken off. In the slick *Caravan of History* (similar to *Vogue* in the United States), only about 10 percent of the ads are entirely in Russian, and they appear mostly towards the end of the magazine. The majority are in English, with some phrases in Russian; French, Spanish, and Italian ads also appear. Aimed largely at women, they stress "the good life": Western cosmetics, perfume, alcohol, cigarettes, lingerie, luxury condos. "I am worth it," "I value quality," etc., are leitmotifs that recur in them. In magazines devoted to cooking or gardening, however, the ads are almost all in Russian.

In 1993, a law was passed stating that, although foreign companies operating in Russia, such as McDonald's, Estée Lauder, Gucci, and Levi Strauss, could have their logos displayed in their native language, they were also required to have their logos prominently displayed in Cyrillic.

❀

## 3. APPROACHING STRANGERS IN PUBLIC TO ASK FOR INFORMATION

To attract someone's attention to ask for directions, for the cost of an item, or about transportation, address the person by saying "Izvi*ni*te, po*zhal*uista," Excuse me, please (**Извини́те, пожа́луйста**), "Ska*zhi*te, po*zhal*uista," Tell me, please (**Скажи́те, пожа́луйста**), or simply "Po*zhal*uista," Please (**Пожа́луйста**). Indeed, "po*zhal*uista," please (**пожа́луйста**), is a most useful Russian word to use to ask for help, to thank someone, or to invite someone to the table.

"Izvi*ni*te," Excuse me (**извини́те**), can be used to attract someone's attention as well as to apologize for some minor transgression. If you are mistaken for a Russian and are approached with a question in Russian, just say, "Izvi*ni*te, ya ne govo*ryu* po-*russ*ki," Excuse me, I don't speak Russian (**Извини́те, я не говорю́ по-ру́сски**).

❀

# 4. AT THE TABLE

If you are invited for dinner at someone's home, expect to be seated at the table. Cocktail parties and buffet dinners where guests eat standing are not common in Russia, although they are becoming more frequent as more Western and other companies conduct business in Russia.

Russian generosity is justly renowned. Even in a dire economy, be prepared for an impressive spread when invited to a Russian home. And no one will mention that half a month's salary has been spent on the meal! In response to the invitation "Pro*shu* k sto*lu*," Please [come] to the table (**Прошу́ к столу́**), everyone will sit down. When Russians join someone who is already eating, or if they leave while others continue to eat, they say "Priy*at*novo appe*tit*a," Bon appétit! (**Прия́тного аппети́та**).

The Russian table setting places the fork on the left side of the plate, the knife and the soup spoon on the right, and the teaspoon above the plate. Dinner-size plates are used for the main course of a dinner, but smaller salad or dessert plates are used for breakfast and lunch. Russians hold the fork in the left hand, the knife in the right. Desserts such as cakes are eaten with a spoon, not with a fork. It is not considered impolite to reach across the table for food (with one's hand or fork), to pick up bread, or to spear a pickle. When not being used, the utensil ends of knives and forks are placed on the plates with the tines of the forks down. To indicate that you have finished a meal, place the fork and knife parallel in the middle of the plate. It is considered polite to leave a bit of food on the plate. If children especially like what they are eating they say, "nyam, nyam"/**ням, ням**. Adults enthuse, "ya*zik* pro*glo*tish"/**язы́к прогло́тишь**, it makes your mouth water, or literally, "you can swallow your tongue." (See also Point 38, "Meals and Mealtimes," and Point 51, "Restaurants.")

# 5. ATTRACTING SOMEONE'S ATTENTION

Since the 1917 Revolution, it has been considered inappropriate to use the Russian terms for Mr., "gospo*din*" (**господи́н**), Mrs. or Miss, "gospo*zha*" (**госпожа́**), and Ladies and Gentlemen, "gospo*da*" (**господа́**). The new terms "grazhda*nin*," "grazh*dan*ka," "*grazh*dane, and "to*varishch*," citizen, citiziness, citizens, and comrade (**граждани́н, гражда́нка, гра́ждане, това́рищ**), were used instead, although they were official and sometimes sounded a bit artificial. In the 1990s, "gospo*din*," Mr. (**господи́н**), "gospo*zha*," Mrs. or Miss (**госпожа́**), and "gospo*da*," Ladies and Gentlemen (**господа́**), appeared to be regaining favor—especially in financial circles—even among Russians. At times, the English words Mr., Mrs., and Miss are used in addressing foreigners.

To attract the attention of a saleslady or a waitress, it is appropriate to call out "*de*vushka," girl (**де́вушка**), to a female aged 15 to 50. In recent years, the words "*pa*ren," fellow (**па́рень**), "molo*doy* chelo*vek*" young man (**молодо́й челове́к**), "muzh*chi*na," man (**мужчи́на**), and "*zhen*shchina," woman (**же́нщина**), have come to be widely used, although educated Russians consider this practice crude, and foreigners should not use the latter two appellations.

❀

# 6. *BABUSHKA, GRANDMOTHER (БАБУШКА)*

A grandmother, more frequently than in the West, lives with one of her children, not only due to the housing shortage, but also because of the closeness of the Russian extended family. Especially if she is retired, a babushka is the main helper in the family, preparing meals, babysitting, shopping, and even assisting with the grandchildren's homework. Grandmothers also act as commentators on social behavior, reprimanding those they consider to be out of line. They can be found in all kinds of weather, sitting on benches in front of their homes in the countryside or at the entrances to apartment buildings in the city.

❁

# 7. BALLET AND THE RUSSIAN THEATER

Although ballet originated in the court of Louis XIV of France, its glory days came when it grew in Russian soil. Empress Elizabeth, Peter the Great's daughter, created a court school in St. Petersburg in the eighteenth century. By Pushkin's day in the nineteenth century, ballet had reached a position of significant artistic importance. In the twentieth century, it was impossible to conceive of a diplomatic mission to Moscow without the requisite evening at the Bolshoi Theater, preferably to see "Lebe*dinoe ozero*," *Swan Lake* (**Лебеди́ное о́зеро**). Tickets to Moscow's Bolshoi Theater or Leningrad's Kirov Theater (now St. Petersburg's Mariinsky Theater) were greatly valued as bribes during much of the Soviet period.

The following appears on a ticket to a Russian performance: the name of the theater, the date of the production, the name of the production (stamped, i.e., not printed, on the ticket), and the location of the seat in the theater. A ticket with "par*ter*," orchestra seats (**партéр**), "*levaya storona*," left side (**лéвая сторонá**), "*ryad* 2," row 2 (**ряд 2**), "*mesto* 16," place 16 (**мéсто 16**), indicates that the ticket is for the left side of the orchestra, row 2, seat 16. "*Pravaya storona*" would send the theatergoer to the right side (**прáвая сторонá**). Other terms used in traditional opera/ballet theaters to designate seats are, in ascending order: seats on the same level as the orchestra seats, but behind and around them (lower boxes)—"benu*ar*" (**бенуáр**); the tier immediately above this level (dress circle)—"bele*tazh*" (**бельэтáж**); the tiers above these two levels—"*yarus*" (**я́рус**); the last balcony (the gallery)—"gale*reya*" (**галерéя**). "*Lozha*" (**лóжа**) indicates that the seat is in a box. Newer theaters designate the less expensive orchestra seats "amfite*atr*" (**амфитеáтр**), and the balcony "bal*kon*" (**балкóн**). (It is wise to be in your seat at the start of a performance; once the performance begins, latecomers are not seated until there is a significant break in the action on stage, or possibly only at the end of the first act. Latecomers are sometimes seated in unoccupied balcony seats until the end of the first act. It is also common for Russians to move into better, unoccupied seats once a performance starts.)

Whereas in the United States there is usually a free theater program full of information about the performance and the cast, plus advertising geared for a theatergoing audience, in Russia there is a minimal charge for a two- or four-page program giving the most essential information—scenes, acts, and cast member names. In both countries, vendors sell more complete—and more expensive—souvenir programs.

In addition to ordinary applause, Russians often express pleasure by rhythmic clapping. Shouts of *Bravo!* and *Brava!* greet popular performers. As elsewhere, favorite performers are presented with flowers. At theaters such as the Bolshoi or the Mariinsky (Kirov), the flowers are presented by ushers on stage, or they are thrown onto the stage by fans. When an orchestra pit does not prevent the fans from approaching the stage, fans hand flowers directly to the performers. While the fans are applauding, frequently the performers themselves will also applaud, signifying appreciation for the audience. As in most of Europe, fans express displeasure by whistling. During intermissions, many theaters have a public room "fo*ye*" (**фойе**) in which theatergoers, arm in arm, promenade, walking round and round the room. Others head for the theater's buffets. Because most evening performances begin at seven o'clock, theatergoers do not have time to eat dinner at home. Open-faced caviar, salami, or smoked fish sandwiches, pastries, and chocolate—washed down with juice or champagne (served in real glasses, as opposed to plastic ones)—help assuage hunger and make the occasion a festive one. When delicacies are scarce elsewhere, they can generally be found at theaters.

When Russians enter a row with people already seated in it, they face those seated rather than the stage, and proceed across the row. To do otherwise, i.e., to face the stage, is considered impolite because one's back side then faces those seated.

Coats, hats, or rubber overshoes may not be worn in the seating area of Russian theaters (or in places such as museums and restaurants).

They must be left at the "garde*rob*," cloakroom (**гардеро́б**). There is no charge for this service, and kind cloakroom attendants have been known to repair a loose "*ve*shalka," loop near the coat collar (**ве́шалка**), that is used to hang up the coat. After the removal of hats and coats, public primping at the mirrors provided in the coatroom is an accepted practice. When the performance is over, people line up to retrieve their coats. To avoid standing in line, patrons frequently rent binoculars at a modest cost, even if they have excellent seats, because returning the binoculars assures a quick move to the front of the coat line. In movie theaters and at sporting events Russians keep their coats on.

# 8. *BANYA*, THE RUSSIAN SAUNA (*БА́НЯ*)

The tradition of the Russian sauna is very old; it is known to have existed in the Middle Ages. Until the 1917 Bolshevik Revolution, almost every Russian village house had its own *banya*, separate from the main house. Eighty percent of the population lived in villages. The *banya* was built close to a water supply such as a river, a lake, or a town well. The air inside a *banya* is heated by wood-burning stoves. Water is boiled in kettles and poured on heated stones. The resulting moist hot air is different from the dry heat of Finnish saunas. In a *banya* people sit or lie naked on benches and beat themselves with a birch or oak switch called a "*ve*nik" (**ве́ник**). To protect their hair, men wear woolen hats, and women, if they can, braid their hair. Men and women take turns using the *banya*. Afterward, people jump into the cold water of a lake or river or roll around in the snow. In another era, Russians were suspicious of people who did not partake of *banyas*. Historian and author Nikolai Karamzin wrote that when the throne was empty during the "Time of Troubles" (1605–1613) after the death of Tsar Boris Godunov and several pretenders claimed to be the rightful tsar, Russians did not believe that the one who actually ruled for a brief period, known as "The False Dmitry," was Russian, because he never went to the *banya*.

Communal baths are located in cities and towns. The demand for them originally came from factories. After bathing, instead of jumping into a lake or river, as in the country, people douse themselves with cold water from a bucket, or in the case of modern *banyas*, from a shower. These types of *banyas* are divided into four parts. People undress in the "pred*b*annik," dressing room (**предба́нник**). There is a "*mo*echnaya," washing room (**мо́ечная**), sometimes called a "dushe*vaya*" (**душева́я**). Afterwards, people head for the "pari*l*ka," the steam room (**пари́лка**). They sit on stone benches (as expected, the higher they choose to sit, the hotter the air) and beat themselves, as described above. The humid air is so hot that one can stay there for only limited periods of time. In the steam room people sit; drink tea, beer, or vodka; play chess; or chat.

At present, even though most apartments have bathrooms, *banyas* continue to enjoy great popularity. This is especially true May through September, when throughout Russia 149 million people cope with no hot water for up to a month while rusty pipes are checked and repaired. Their attraction lies in the fact that not only do they represent a source for cleanliness, but perhaps even more importantly, they provide a place for people to gather for social pleasure. Upon returning from a *banya*, Russians are greeted with "S *lyokh*kim *pa*rom!"/**с лёгким па́ром**, congratulating the person on the expedition and trusting that the "steam," par/**пар**, was healthful. By extension, one who has just taken a shower or bath may be greeted in the same manner.

❀

# 9. BRIBERY AND *BLAT*, "PULL" (*БЛАТ*)

Bribery has always been a frequent practice in Russia (as in many other countries). Even during the time of the tsars, Russian officials excelled at bribery. In the nineteenth-century satirical play, *The Inspector General*, one of Nikolai Gogol's characters accuses another of "taking more than is your due"; he does not criticize him for bribery as such. "Ne pod*ma*zhesh, ne po*e*desh," If you don't oil [i.e., give a bribe], you cannot start your journey (**Не подма́жешь, не пое́дешь**), is an old Russian proverb. Bribes are offered to get a child into a university, to obtain a good job, to help a business, and to avoid army service.

During the time of Stalin, bribery was less widespread than at other times in Russia's history. Laws are strictly enforced under despots. If there is a choice between "life" or "a bribe," most people choose life and avoid bribes. Since the 1960s, bribery has become more prevalent, because laws are less strictly enforced. Accusations have been made that bribery and corruption exist even in the very highest circles of Russian society. In its 1998 *Corruption Perception Index*, Transparency International ranked Russia 76th among 85 countries (with 85 being the worst).

*Blat*, which can be best translated as "pull," "influence," or "connections," has always been important in Russia. As in many other countries, it is not important what you know, but who you know. Even in everyday life it is almost impossible to accomplish something if you do not have contacts—"svo*ya* ru*ka*" (**своя́ рука́**)—in the right places. Want a ticket to a special theater performance, a permit for the opening of a business venture or for construction? It is absolutely necessary to know where to turn, and what "token"—not a bribe, but a souvenir, or a gift of appreciation—to present to whom. Depending on what "favor" is needed, these "gifts" can vary—a package of cigarettes (Marlboro is the most popular), toys, a bottle of Scotch or bourbon, cosmetics, a computer, or a ticket to the USA. It is possible that people you meet at first in formal, "bribetaking" situations may with time become your personal "friends" and that you will exchange favors on a regular basis.

❀

# 10. THE CALENDAR

Like the European calendar, the Russian calendar week starts with Monday and ends with Sunday. The names of the days reflect this fact: "*vtor*nik," Tuesday (**вто́рник**), comes from "vto*roy*," (**второ́й**) second [day of the week]. Russian calendars generally are aligned up and down, not left to right. Pocketbook-size calendars with a tear-off page per day are popular in Russia. The calendars are labeled "for women," "for schoolchildren," etc. For each day there is reading material of interest to those for whom the calendars are intended.

Since 1918 Russia has followed the Gregorian calendar; previously the Julian calendar was used. Consequently, the October Revolution, which took place on October 25, 1917, by the Julian calendar, after 1918 was celebrated on November 7th. The Russian Orthodox Church continues to follow the Julian calendar; hence Christmas is celebrated not on December 25th, but on January 7th, by Russian Christians.

❀

# 11. CELEBRATIONS AND HOLIDAYS

Russians have always loved to celebrate. During tsarist times, the holidays were associated with the Russian Orthodox religion, the reign of the Romanovs, and the special personal days of the reigning tsar's family. Life in the village revolved around the church calendar. Peasants plowed on St. George's Day in May and picked apples on Transfiguration Day in August. After the October 1917 Revolution, religious holidays were frequently replaced by official secular holidays.

Of the church holidays, Easter (*Pas*kha/**Пácха**), in contrast to the West's Christmas, is the most significant. Before the 1917 Bolshevik Revolution, Easter followed Lent, a seven-week period of strict fasting. Today, fasting is again becoming common, especially during the week before Easter. Even the nonreligious observe Easter. In the evening people begin to gather in churches. The traditional Easter foods, "ku*lich*," an Easter cake similar to sweet bread (**кулѝч**), "*pas*kha," an Easter dessert similar to cheesecake (**пácха**), and colored Easter eggs, known as "*kra*shennie *yay*tsa" (**крáшенные яӗ̆ца**, or in Ukrainian "*pis*anki," **пѝсанки**), are presented to the priests to be blessed. The official celebration of Easter begins at midnight on Saturday and continues into Sunday; A festive service is conducted, and the entire congregation, carrying icons, banners, and incense, follows the priests in a procession around the church. After midnight, and whenever believers meet the next day, they kiss three times and say in Church Slavonic (not Russian) "Khri*s*tos vo*s*kre*s*e," Christ has risen (**Христо́с воскре́се**), and the reply is "Vo*i*stinu vo*s*kre*s*e," Truly He has risen (**Вои́стину воскре́се**). After the church service, the fast is broken with a sumptuous feast.

Those who do not themselves go to church can watch Easter and Christmas services, led by the Patriarch of Moscow and All Russia, on television.

Other secular and religious holidays are:

| | | | |
|---|---|---|---|
| January 1–2 | New Year's Day | *No*viy god | **Но́вый год** |
| January 7 | Christmas (Russian Orthodox Church) | Rozhdest*vo* | **Рождество́** |
| March 8 | International Women's Day | Mezhduna*rod*niy *zhen*skiy den | **Междунаро́д-ный же́нский день** |
| May 1–2 | May Day | *Pra*zdnik ves*ni* i tru*da* | **Пра́здник весны́ и труда́** |
| May 9 | Victory Day | Den Po*b*edi | **День Побе́ды** |
| June 12 | Independence Day of Russia | Den Neza*v*isimosti Ros*sii* | **День Незави́симости Росси́и** |
| November 7 | Anniversary of the October 1917 Revolution | Godov*shchi*na Ok*ty*abrskoy revo*lyu*tsii 1917 *go*da | **Годовщи́на Октя́брьской револю́ции 1917 го́да** |
| October 7 | Constitution Day of the Russian Republic | Den Konstit*ut*sii Ros*si*yskoy Feder*at*isii | **День Конститу́ции Росси́йской Федера́ции** |

Following the 1917 Revolution, Christmas was no longer celebrated. It became an official holiday again in Russia only in 1993. Some offices and institutions celebrate both holidays, Russian Orthodox Christmas on January 7 and Western Christmas on December 25.

Like many European cultures, Russia has the equivalent of a Santa Claus to help celebrate New Year's, and perhaps again soon, Christmas. "Ded M*oroz*," Grandfather Frost (**Дед Моро́з**), is generally taller than Santa and may wear either a blue or a red costume. At holiday parties, or "*yol*ki" (**ёлки**), he is frequently accompanied by "Sneg*u*rochka," Snowmaiden (**Снегу́рочка**), who helps him distribute presents. The name for the holiday party, "*yol*ka," comes from the Russian word for a fir tree. Peter the Great introduced the custom of decorating trees for the Christmas and New Year's holidays after his visit to Europe in the eighteenth century.

March 8, International Women's Day or simply Women's Day, is celebrated in Russia, but barely gets mentioned in U.S. newspapers. All women are honored on this day. On the day prior to the holiday, males give cards, gifts, and/or flowers to their fellow students, colleagues, and co-workers. On the actual holiday, families and friends gather, and gifts are proffered to the females present. While there is no equivalent holiday for men, women frequently congratulate and give cards and/or gifts to male acquaintances on February 23rd, known in the former Soviet Union as "Den So*vet*skoy *A*rmii i Vo*e*nno-Mor*s*kovo *Flo*ta," Soviet Army and Navy Day (**День Сове́тской А́рмии и Вое́нно-Морско́го Фло́та**). It is now called "Defenders of the Fatherland Day," Den za*shchi*tnika O*te*chestva/**День защи́тника оте́чества**.

As is common in the United States where the observed day of a holiday is changed in order to give workers an extended weekend, a holiday in Russia may also be observed on another day. Moreover, if a holiday falls on a Tuesday, workers may be given the option of working on the preceding Saturday, so that they can be off the next Saturday, Sunday, Monday, and Tuesday. Russians who have country homes, or dachas (see Point 17), particularly appreciate these extended holidays. Anyone traveling to Russia on business should check the calendar for holidays to confirm any days that the business offices may be closed.

※

## 12. THE CIRCUS

The circus is a popular form of entertainment in Russia. The Russian circus emphasizes talent and skill, and most popular acts feature acrobats, trapeze artists, clowns, and animals. Bears and horses appear most frequently, but elephants, tigers, lions, dogs, and even pigs and cats, are also featured.

Moscow has two circus buildings and two troupes. The older circus, recently renovated, features animal acts; the newer one, near Moscow State University, is famous for its trapeze artists, who fly high above the spectators. Russian circus performers always use safety nets.

When Russians want to indicate that things have gone out of whack, they say, simply, "tsirk!" circus! (**цирк**), "nu i tsirk!" it's a circus, all right! (**ну и цирк!**), or "nastoyashchiy tsirk!" a real circus! (**настоя́щно и цирк!**).

## 13. CLOTHING

Clothing styles in Russia are in a state of flux. In general, Russians are more conservative in their dress than Americans. For example, in the 1970s, when pantsuits were popular in Europe and in America, young Russian women who wore them were severely criticized by the older generation. To this day, except for sports events, shorts are not considered to be appropriate apparel, even in the hotter southern regions of Russia, nor would high school or college students wear sweats to classes. Likewise, people dress in more somber colors than in the West. Having said this, however, it must be noted that in the 2000s, a wide variety of clothing is seen on Russian streets and in the workplace, because the demand for clothing is greater than the supply. People buy what is available and wear it, and the results may be bewildering. A secretary in an office might be wearing jeans—or a dress Westerners might consider more appropriate for evening wear. In Russian institutions of higher learning, students tend to dress more formally than those in the West. Women wear attractive dresses, hose, and high heels; men, dark dress pants or black jeans and dark shoes. In winter, many Russian women, and by no means just the rich ones, wear gorgeous fur coats and hats. Russians often wear the same outfit for a number of days in a row.

Since the 1990s, as Western clothing has become more available and affordable, newly rich Russians, especially in big cities, have been seen wearing fashionable quality clothing. Recognizable Western brands (Calvin Klein, Liz Claiborne, and Tommy Hilfiger) are especially prized. Prior to the 1990s, quality clothing was scarce in Russia. Visitors wearing Western dress frequently received stares because of their fashionable clothing. Russians sometimes offered to buy the sylish Western clothing, referred to as "fir*ma*," **фирма́** in Russian. This was especially true of the famous brand-name items, which have snob appeal and which in some circles enhance the owner's social status. Sometimes Russians refer to Western visitors as "fir*ma*."

From the 1970s to the early 1990s, of all Western apparel, jeans and clothing made from denim, were considered to be the height of fashion and an indication that the owner had "made it." Russians dressed in the latest fashion, "o*d*eti v fir*mu*," **оде́ты в фирму́**, are seen more and more in the larger cities. Those interested go to a form of flea market, "veshchev*ie rin*ki"/**вещевы́е ры́нки** or "*me*lkoop*t*ovie *rin*ki"/**ме́лкооптóвые ры́нки**, for inexpensive, but currently fashionable, clothing and shoes from Poland, Turkey, China, Korea, and Vietnam or to "secondhand" stores for items from the United States and Germany. (See Point 56, "Shopping.")

In addition to the popularity of quality Western clothing, there is a growing appreciation of Russia's own fashion industry. It is also true that many Russians throughout their lives sew their own clothes or rely on a dressmaker or a tailor ("port*noi*/**портнóй**) to sew their clothing. "Do*ma mo*di," Houses of fashion (**Домá мóды**), can be found in the larger cities of Russia. Valentin Yudashkin and Slava Zaitsev (who designed for Raisa Gorbacheva) are probably the best known of the Russian designers. Responding to the new market economy of the 1990s and early 2000s, Russia's ready-to-wear industry is also experiencing an upsurge. Clothes with a "Made in Russia" label can now be found in American stores.

Foreigners who do not want to draw attention to themselves for security reasons should avoid bright colors, should not wear baseball caps (although Russians will be seen wearing them), and should not carry knapsacks. Students who are Russia bound are advised not to walk down public streets smiling!

In churches and monasteries, slacks for women are not considered proper attire, and heads must be covered. Men's hats, on the other hand, should be removed. It is considered rude for both sexes to walk around with hands in pockets.

❁

## 14. THE COLORS BLUE AND BROWN

Russians differentiate between shades of blue. Dark blue is "*siniy*"/**си́ний**, and light blue is "golu*boy*"/**голубо́й** (the latter is a Russian slang term for a homosexual male). The color brown has its own peculiarities. "Ko*rich*neviy"/**Кори́чневый** means "brown"; however, this word is never used to describe eye color. If someone's eyes are dark brown (almost black), they are referred to as "*chor*nie"/**чёрные**; light brown eyes are "*ka*rie"/**ка́рие**.

❁

## 15. COMPLIMENTS

Americans are known throughout the world for their compliments. Russians, though less outgoing to strangers, also use expressions that convey praise. "Molo*dets*!," Well done! [literally, Great fellow!] (**Молоде́ц**), is said to people of all ages and genders, not just to males. Russian and American reactions to compliments vary. When an American is paid a compliment, the typical reaction is to say "thanks";

a Russian, on the other hand, looks for an excuse to diminish the compliment. "Oh, thank you, but I've had this dress for ten years." In spite of such responses, compliments are much appreciated.

※

# 16. CRAFTS

Russia is renowned for the wealth of its arts and crafts. Most famous are its "*pa*lekh," lacquer boxes (**па́лех**) and brooches from the four villages of Palekh, Mstyora, Kholui, and Fedoskino; "khokhlo*ma*," painted woodenware (**хохлома́**) bowls, plates, spoons; Zhostovo trays; Pavlovoposadskie wool shawls; Orenburg shawls made from mohair; Gzhel pottery, and Dymkov toys. Add to this list the ever popular Russian *matryoshkas* (nesting dolls), samovars; balalaikas; embroidered linens; carvings of bone, wood, and stone; and wooden toys, with moving parts, of people or animals, and you will understand why there is never a need for a Russian to give a present "Made in Hong Kong." The items mentioned above are so valued that a Russian will appreciate receiving them as gifts from a foreign visitor, in case you did not bring anything appropriate from home.

※

# 17. *DACHA,* COUNTRY HOUSE (ДА́ЧА)

Every Russian family living in the city strives to have its own dacha, and the Soviet government allowed many applicants to use government–owned land for dachas without a charge. Dachas provide a way to raise produce and escape from the city, with its bureaucracy and other types of constraints. Although there was some variation by region, up until 1991 the maximum allowable size of the dacha area to be gardened ("sa*do*viy u*cha*stok"/**садо́вый уча́сток**) was 720 square yards; the maximum size for buildings, 30 square yards; and the maximum size for a patio, 12 square yards. In 1991 the limitations regarding the size and the quality of dachas were eliminated, and local authorities were given the right to set the maximum allowable area to be gardened. Russians took advantage of the new regulation, and today the results can be seen in the attractive houses that have sprung up throughout Russia. In 1993 more than half of Russia's population had some access to a dacha, and 20 million families have plots of land in the country. Russian dachas are now more and more likely to attract long-term dwellers, especially retired people who make them their permanent homes. Younger people are less favorably inclined toward dachas—the lack of indoor plumbing and telephones, plus the hard work connected with gardening, no doubt play a role. A new development is that Russia's newly rich "*novie rus*skie"/**но́вые ру́сские** have taken to building expensive private residences, "kot*t*edzhi"/**котте́джи**, on plots outside the big cities for their pleasure, sometimes making them their permanent residences.

The gardens around dachas are a significant source of food to supplement what can be obtained in the city and help Russians to economize. During the summer, tomatoes, cucumbers, zucchini, onions, garlic, lettuce, all kinds of herbs, and early potatoes add to the variety of food available in the stores. In the fall, potatoes, cabbage, carrots, and onions are stored in cool storage places, pickled, or otherwise preserved. Home canning adds considerably to the winter diet.

Dachas are also a source of fruits and berries, even in very cold areas. Apple trees, plum trees, and sometimes pear or cherry trees are grown. Strawberries are very popular in early summer; gooseberries, black and red currants, and raspberries in midsummer; and "oble*p*ikha"/**облепи́ха** (orange seabuckthorn berries) in late summer. In autumn, mountain ash berries are popular.

Russians differentiate between a garden where vegetables and berries grow, an "ogo*rod*"/**огоро́д**, and one primarily dedicated to flowers and trees, a "sad"/**сад**. If the garden contains both vegetables and flowers, "sad"/**сад** is used.

# 18.  DATING, MARRIAGE, AND DIVORCE

Only in recent years has limited dating started in Russian high schools. Generally, youngsters rarely date until they reach age 16. During the last two years of high school, life is filled with studies and preparation for college exams. Moreover, any public display of affection between a male and a female student is likely to land the Romeo and Juliet in the principal's office. However, students attending the less academically demanding vocational and technical schools become romantically involved more readily. Nevertheless, while still in school, youngsters generally do things in groups, such as go to films and discos, gather for parties at home, stroll in parks, or meet at the entrances to apartment buildings.

Real dating begins in college. The verb used for "going out" is "vstre*chat*sya"/**встречáться**, which literally means "to meet." Students gather at dances usually organized by the university's social club. Sometimes these dances are preceded by a film or some other kind of presentation such as a lecture. Working-class youth meet at events organized by clubs connected with factories. City-sponsored discotheques are also popular. Another popular meeting place is the movie theater. Since the mid-1990s, with the appearance of inexpensive restaurants, cafes and such have also become popular meeting places. Likewise, each town, or each region in cities, has a special street, informally understood to be "the street of strolling." Here youngsters gather: pairs of girls walk arm-in-arm, boys in noisy groups gather around them—and friendships and romances begin.

Russians must be 18 years old to get married. Usually, after a young person starts earning money, nothing can stop him or her from marrying. Young men typically marry between 22 and 26. Although girls used to marry two or three years earlier, current statistics indicate a tendency for females to marry even younger, at 18 or 17 (with special permission). An increase in the number of common-law couples is also evident. A couple must obtain a wedding certificate. The waiting period for this certificate is three months, but the waiting period is considerably reduced if the bride is pregnant.

Wedding certificates are obtained from ZAGS, "(Ot*del*) *za*pisi *ak*tov grazh*dan*skovo sosto*ya*niya," Civil Registry Office (**Отде́л за́писи а́ктов гражда́нского состоя́ния**), or in special Wedding Palaces, "D*vor*tsi brakosoche*ta*niya"/**Дворцы́ бракосочета́ния**. Prior to the 1990s, most Russians were married in such Wedding Palaces. Since then there has been an increase in the number of weddings taking place in churches. As in the United States, to be legally complete, the ceremony in a church must be supplemented by a certificate of marriage issued by the appropriate governmental entity. The Russian Orthodox wedding ceremony is known for the special wedding crowns that are held above the bride's and groom's heads, as was described in the wedding of Levin and Kitty in Leo Tolstoy's *Anna Karenina*.

After the official wedding ceremony, the couple traditionally visits historically significant places, where they leave bouquets of flowers. In Moscow, the most popular choices are the Grave of the Unknown Soldier near the Kremlin, Sparrow Hills near Moscow State University with its impressive view of Moscow, and, after it was opened in 1995, Victory Park (Park Po*bed*i/**Парк Побе́ды**, also referred to as Po*klo*nnaya Go*ra*/**Покло́нная Гора́**). In St. Petersburg, married couples can be seen at the Rostral Columns by the spit of Vasilevsky Island, the statue of the Bronze Horseman (Peter the Great), the Field of Mars, and Piskaryovskoe Memorial Cemetery. The newlyweds ride in a car with big wedding rings on the roof, a doll on the front of the hood, and decorations of flowers, ribbons, and balloons.

A wedding feast concludes the day's festivities. This feast takes place in an apartment, a restaurant, or in special banquet halls. Guests sit at tables laden with the best that the parents of the groom and the bride can afford (the two families share the expenses). Prior to eating, the groom's father toasts the couple. Appetizers and numerous meat and fish dishes are set on the tables or offered by servers to the guests. During the meal, many toasts are made. Frequent shouts of "*gorko*," bitter (**го́рько**), can be heard, which is a signal that the groom should kiss the bride to "sweeten" life. Russians love music and singing, and songs resound throughout the celebration.

After the wedding, if a room can be found for them to squeeze into, the young couple typically will move in with one of the parents, due to a shortage of apartments. Only in the mid-1990s have some apartments become available in cities for rent or purchase. However, they are frightfully expensive, and it is unusual for a young couple to be able to afford one of their own.

The divorce rate in Russia is very high, 30 percent (almost as high as in the United States), and it is rising. Statistics published in Russian newspapers indicate that from 1990 to 1992 the divorce rate increased by 15 percent. The reasons for the high rate are numerous: lack of privacy because of the housing shortage, alcoholism, personality and cultural differences, sexual incompatibility, and adultery.

# 19. "DO YOU NOT KNOW?"

The Russian way of asking a question is, instead of saying, "Please tell me where the Mariinsky Theater is located," to ask, "Do you not know where the Mariinsky Theater is located?" If the person responding to the question is an out-of-towner, unfamiliar with St. Petersburg's theaters, or unaware that the Kirov Theater has reverted to its original name, the Mariinsky—having the question posed in the negative makes it easier to answer "No, I do not" and not feel guilty about it.

# 20. EDUCATION AND UPBRINGING, OBRAZOVANIE AND VOSPITANIE (*ОБРАЗОВÁНИЕ* AND *ВОСПИТÁНИЕ*)

The Soviet government designed its educational policies to make sure that a person received not just an education, "obrazovanie"/ **образовáние**, at school, but also "vospitanie"/**воспитáние**—moral upbringing and good breeding. Guided by the ideology of Marxism-Leninism, schools expected students not only to get good grades but to be active members of the Young Octobrist, Pioneer, and Komsomol organizations (See Point 39, "Milestones"), wear their uniforms, love Lenin and the Motherland, and hate the Soviet Union's enemies. World War II was to be remembered and the school area's war veterans to be honored at school events. Great effort was exerted to instill in the students a love for physical labor. On the Saturday "sub*bot*nik"/**суббо́тник** before Lenin's birthday (April 22), youngsters in cities were supposed to volunteer their time, helping with clean-up projects and aiding recycling efforts. In rural areas, schoolchildren helped with agricultural chores on collective farms (kolkhozes). Respect for teachers (elders in general), discipline, and the needs of the collective (as opposed to the individual) were stressed. Since the early 1990s, much has changed in educational policy.

School always starts on September 1, unless that date falls on a Sunday, in which case opening day is September 2. Children enter the first grade at age 6 and generally attend school until they have completed the eleventh grade, although only nine grades are compulsory. Students generally walk to the neighborhood school. Elementary, middle-, and high-school students study together in one, multistoried building rather than in separate buildings as is common in American schools. From the first day of first grade, students are assigned to a homeroom, which they will keep through the eleventh grade. Schools in populated, newer areas of the country sometimes have as many as six or seven homerooms per grade level. Students are divided into homerooms, or classes, of 30–40 students. Each homeroom receives its own letter (in Cyrillic, of course), 1A, 1B, and so forth. There is mingling among homerooms, but real closeness exists among the students within one homeroom. In a society in which not *what* you know but *who* you know is of prime importance, the friendships forged "na stu*den*cheskoy ska*me*," at a student desk (**студе́нческой скамье́**), cannot be overestimated.

A system of special schools, "spetsi*al*nie *shkoli*"/"spets*shkoli*" (**специа́льные шко́лы** or **спецшко́лы**), exists for economics, mathematics, art, and foreign languages. It may take students more than an hour to reach one of these schools. A student who attends a special

English school will begin studying English daily in the second grade in groups of 10 to 15 students. By the end of the eleventh grade he or she will be nearly proficient in the language.

After the ninth grade, students may leave their general secondary school to complete the last two years in a vocational-technical school, where emphasis is on preparing students for skilled or semiskilled jobs in industry, agriculture, or office work.

Prior to the early 1990s even students not enrolled in a vocational-technical school, but in a general secondary or a special school, were required during their last two years to spend one day a week learning a skill such as sewing, house painting, or meat cutting.

Classes generally begin at 8:30 AM and last until 1:30 or 2:30 PM, six days a week. However, in the late 1980s, many schools started a five-day week, citing parental pressure to give children, especially in the early grades, a two-day weekend. In some localities, because of a lack of school buildings, students attend school in two shifts; the second group begins classes around 1:30 PM and ends at 6:30 or 7:00 PM.

The 1990s saw other changes in secondary education that continued into the 2000s. Whereas school formerly was compulsory, free, and co-educational, some private schools "*cha*stnie *shko*li," "gim*nazii*," or "*litsei*" (**частные школы, гимназии, лицеи**) now charge for education and limit enrollment to only girls or only boys. Education remains compulsory until age 15. Private schools offer a wider curriculum than that found in state schools and hire the best teachers available, including native speakers for foreign languages. Church schools, illegal since the Bolshevik Revolution, are reappearing.

In Russian schools rote memorization plays a more significant role in the educational process than in the West. A delightful result of this practice are the many poems that Russians can recite by memory. Students too frequently, however, were expected merely to write down and retell what they heard in lectures. Since the 1990s, however, the ability to discuss and analyze has become more important. Students are being asked to express their own opinions and come up with creative projects. Teaching and testing in Russian schools and colleges are more frequently oral rather than written, in contrast to Western practice. The whispering of answers and the use of crib sheets is not considered to be the moral transgression that it is in American culture. This whispering is a bonding experience among friends and a vote against authority.

To be admitted into an institution of higher learning, or a "VUZ"/**ВУЗ**, a Russian youngster must take both a written and an oral examination during the summer after graduation. The importance of this test can best be appreciated if one realizes that the application process does not include letters of recommendation from teachers, high school grade point average, standardized test scores, or an applicant's essay. During their last year of high school students choose a profession, concentrate on the courses connected with that specialty to the exclusion of other courses, frequently study with a "repe*tit*or," tutor (**репети́тор**), or attend preparatory classes at their intended institute for a charge, and try their hardest on the exam. Unlike the United States, where a student may apply to as many as ten colleges, a Russian student generally applies to only one. Competition for the best-known institutions of higher learning is extremely stiff. Those who are not selected enter the work force (the importance of vocational training cannot be underestimated). Some students continue to pursue their goal of higher education by seeking admission to evening or extension classes.

When a "stu*dent*," student (**студе́нт**), is admitted to a "universi*tet*," university (**университе́т**), or an "insti*tut*," institute (**институ́т**), he or she becomes part of a group, much like the pupils in elementary through high school. The student has already chosen his or her specialty, hence most of the courses are compulsory, with few electives. Depending on the field of specialization, the years of study range from four to six. In the final year, the student must write and defend a thesis. Upon graduation, the degree earned is somewhat higher than a bachelor's degree.

Tuition previously was free at all institutions of higher learning. Since the late 1990s, however, tracks exist within government institutions for students who do not pay and those who do—from $1000 to $5000 per year. All private institutions of higher learning charge tuition. Cafeteria meals are subsidized by the institution, if it has been able to raise funds for this purpose. Students whose grades are A and B, or who are especially needy, receive a small stipend. To supplement it, many students work part-time.

After graduate study, or "aspiran*tura*" (**аспиранту́ра**), which generally lasts three years, graduates receive a "kandi*dat* na*uk*" (**кандида́т нау́к**), or a candidate of sciences degree, somewhat similar to a master's degree. (In the sciences it may actually be the equivalent of a master's degree.) Additional research and publication is required to be awarded a doctor of sciences, or a "*dok*tor na*uk*" (**до́ктор нау́к**), typically referred to as a "dokto*rant*" (**доктора́нт**). It is more difficult to obtain and more prestigious than an American Ph.D., requiring major original contributions to one's specialized area.

❀

## 21. FAMILY

Traditionally in Russia, especially in the countryside, extended families lived together: grandparents, children, and grandchildren. Even now three generations live together under the same roof 20 percent of the time. Sometimes this is the result of the lack of apartments, sometimes it is the result of close family ties. Most of the time, families try to obtain apartments in the same apartment complex or in close proximity to each other. Members of a family usually rely strongly on each other. People feel safe with their families, just as they do with truly close friends. The need for reliance on one's family played an especially strong role during the Stalin years, when denunciations to the KGB (see Point 29, "Gulag") to obtain a better apartment or a desired job, for example, were common practice. The outcome was distrust of anyone other than one's nearest and dearest. The closeness and warmth of so many Russian families has been commented on by visitors who have been able to penetrate beyond the "tourist" level during their stay in Russia.

The typical Russian family consists of four people: a "muzh," husband (**муж**), "zhe*na*," wife (**жена́**), and two children, a "doch/*doch*ka," daughter (**дочь/до́чка**), and/or a "sin," son (**сын**), and may include grandparents if they are still living: a "*de*dushka," grandfather (**де́душка**), and a "*ba*bushka," grandmother (**ба́бушка**). The terms for brother and

sister are "brat"/**брат** and "se*stra*"/**сестра́**. Cousins are also frequently referred to as "brat"/**брат** and "se*stra*"/**сестра́**, instead of the formal names
"dvo*yu*rodniy brat"/**двою́родный брат** and "dvo*yu*rodnaya se*stra*/
**двою́родная сестра́**. This is especially common if one is an only child
and does not have a brother or a sister. To indicate that "brat"/**брат** and
"se*stra*"/**сестра́** refer to one's real brother or sister, "rod*noy* brat"/**родно́й
брат** and "rod*naya* se*stra*"/**родна́я сестра́** are used.

During the Soviet period most women worked outside the home.
Although there were exceptions, women also did the majority of work
connected with maintaining a home and a family—shopping, cooking,
cleaning, and taking care of the children. There seems to be a movement
among the younger generation for men to be more helpful in a family
setting unless they have to work at numerous jobs to make ends meet,
as many have since the economic disaster of August 1998. A specific
change is that since the appearance of the rich "new Russians," there are
wives who do not work outside the home, a rarity in Russia.

❀

# 22. FIBBING, VRAN*YO* (*ВРАНЬЁ*)

Every culture has a different attitude and explanation for a fib, which in
Russian is referred to as "vran*yo*"/**враньё**. A more serious moral transgression than a "white lie," Russians use it, for example, when they do not
want to admit a shortcoming in themselves, other people, or their country. For example, when asked why there were no handicap-accessible
ramps to restaurants, theaters, etc., Intourist guides used to answer that
invalids preferred to stay in the privacy of their apartments, even though
they were quite aware that their country provided no arrangements for
handicapped people.

❀

## 23. FLOWERS

Flowers have always played a large role in Russian social life. They are presented to visitors and relatives as they arrive or leave. When going to someone's house as a guest, flowers are almost obligatory. Be aware of traditional associations connected with flowers. For example, flowers in even numbers are appropriate only for funerals; uneven numbers are offered in other situations. The colors of flowers also have connotations: white—innocence, red—love, yellow—sadness and betrayal. Generally roses are not given to men, gladioluses are. Carnations are traditionally associated with the Bolshevik Revolution, and on November 7th carnations were frequently given to veterans of the 1917 Revolution and World War II.

In the 1980s, the flower industry became one of the first private enterprises. In large cities flowers are now sold the whole year round—at the metro and train stations, at underground street crossings, and in front of large stores and cemeteries. The most popular flowers are carnations and roses. In the spring one can find tulips, irises, and daffodils; in the summer there are peonies, daisies, and gladioluses. Fall finds dahlias and chrysanthemums being sold. In addition to the flowers grown in hothouses or in individual gardens, Russians are very fond of flowers found in the fields and forests: lilies of the valley, forget-me-nots, and field daisies. Russians also love flowering bushes, especially lilacs, jasmine (similar to mock orange), and trees like the bird cherry. Houseplants, "*kom*natnie tsve*ti*"/**кómнатные цветы́**, are also prevalent in Russian homes and apartments.

## 24. FOREIGNERS

Russians have an ambivalent attitude toward foreigners. During the reign of Peter the Great (1682–1725), credited with opening a "window to Europe," representatives of six countries served in Russia. Foreigners were invited to Russia as soldiers and generals to serve in the military, as engineers and architects to build new cities, as scientists and doctors to develop science and medicine, as scholars to teach in schools and tutor in private households, and as artists to entertain the nobility. Many Russians considered anything foreign to be superior. Foreign goods were sought and foreign literature was imitated. For many decades during the nineteenth century the Russian nobility strove to live like the French nobility—they spoke French at home, wore French fashions, and built and decorated their homes in the French manner. French was the first language of Aleksandr Pushkin, Russia's most beloved poet. Pushkin's Russian peasant nanny was the one who taught him Russian.

There were those in Russian society, however, who resented this bowing to the West. In the nineteenth century two camps formed: Westernizers and Slavophiles. The former, of which Ivan Turgenev was an adherent, felt that Russia as a part of Europe should follow the European model in its development, rationalism, and materialism. Slavophiles felt that Russia had its own destiny, and that Russia's strength lay in the Orthodox Church, autocracy, and the peasant communes. These two divergent outlooks on the West and Russia's roots are still influential in present-day Russian intellectual thought and political life. Mikhail Gorbachev and Boris Yeltsin belong to the Westernizer tradition; the conservative writers Valentin Rasputin and Aleksandr Solzhenitsyn are part of the Slavophile tradition.

Notwithstanding the adulation frequently shown to everything foreign, a negative attitude toward foreigners also exists. Xenophobia is reflected in the negative way foreigners are presented in Russian opera (e.g., *The Tsar's Bride*), in Russian literature, and in the attitude that they can (should) be taken advantage of in financial transactions. During Stalin's time, any evidence of interest in and respect toward Western intellectual thought, art, or fashion could cost the offender his or her life.

Admiration and fear continues to exist in Russian society. On the one hand foreigners are sought out for the Western currency they possess. But on the other hand, there is resentment of the fact that there are doors open to them because of their currency. During the NATO bombing of Serbia and Kosovo in 1999, many Russians showed anti-NATO, but especially anti-American, feelings. Heartfelt sympathy was shown to Americans after the September 2001 terrorist attacks on New York and Washington. In the business sphere, foreigners are invited to invest in Russia through ads in newspapers and magazines; however, their legal rights remain in flux. Pro-Western views are likely to be held by younger, well-educated people studying or working in big cities in the fields of economics, computer science, or any advanced disciplines. People living in the provinces, war veterans, and working people are more likely to be anti-Western.

English-speaking foreigners who wish to live in the larger cities in Russia will find that since the early 1990s, a service industry caters to them. Numerous newspapers are published in English, there are radio stations broadcast in English, and CNN can be received in many apartments and hotels. The danger of such an "all-English world" for foreigners who choose not to be involved with the Russian world is possible isolation from the country and its citizens.

## 25. FRIEND, *DRUG ["DROOG"] (ДРУГ)*, AND WAYS TO DENOTE FRIENDSHIP

The Russian language has a number of words for "friend." However, there are significant differences in meaning, depending on the closeness of the relationship. An acquaintance is a "zna*komiy*" **знако́мый**. "Pri*yatel*"/**Прия́тель** is the term for people with whom one has a closer relationship. The closest relationships are expressed by the terms "drug" [pronounced "droog"], friend, male or female (**друг**), and "po*drug*a," female friend (**подру́га**). (However, if a male refers to a female as his "po*drug*a," it implies that they are on intimate terms.) One feels blessed to have three or four such friends. For a Russian, having a close friend carries a significantly more important role than for those in most other countries. In times of difficulties and hostility under the tsars and the dictators, a devoted friend, who could be truly trusted and from whom one could receive support and understanding, was a genuine treasure.

Such friends can be called on the telephone at any time during the day or night, money can be borrowed from them, and a telephone call is not required before a house visit.

There are no close equivalents to the terms "boyfriend" and "girlfriend" in Russian. In a dating situation, the words "mo1o*doy* che1o*vek*," young man /**молодо́й челове́к**, and "*pa*ren," fellow/**па́рень** are used for boyfriend, and "*de*vushka," girl/**де́вушка** for girlfriend, although more and more frequently the English terms "boyfriend" and "girlfriend" are being used, especially by the younger generation, but even by Russians who do not know English. These words appear frequently in Russian magazines. On the cover of a November 2000 magazine, for example, the word "boyfriend" appears transliterated into Cyrillic letters: **бойфре́нд**. If a live-in boyfriend or girl-friend is involved, the adjective "neras*pi*san-niy," officially not registered, i.e., not married (**нерасписанный**), will be added. Two additional terms for "lover" are "so*zh*itel"/**сожи́тель** (one who shares living quarters) and one who most likely does not: "lyu*bov*nik"/**любо́вник**. A new term for "a hot young male" in the 2000s is "*pe*rets," literally, pepper (**пе́рец**). Until the 1990s, live-in situations occurred considerably less frequently than in the West, primarily due to the lack of available apartments. Lately, as apartments have become more available for rent or purchase, there is an increase in such live-in situations for those who have money.

⚜

# 26. GESTURES

Russians, as a rule, are not as demonstrative with gestures as some other European peoples. They tend to be similar to Americans. Moreover, many gestures, such as twirling a finger at one's temple to indicate that a person is crazy, rubbing three fingers together to convey the idea of the need for money, or holding up a thumb as a sign of approval, are the same for Russians and Americans. A certain number of signs do exist, of course, that are not common to both countries. Only recently have

Russians begun to understand and use the Western sign for victory, i.e., two fingers held up like a "V." In Russian films, which are becoming more available to viewers in the West, one sees the gesture that indicates the desire to have a drink, i.e., the flipping of fingers against the lower part of the jaw.

❀

## 27. GIFTS

Russians, as a rule, are very generous people. The old adage is that if you compliment a Russian on an item he or she is wearing or has in the apartment, that item is likely to be given to you. Russians like to give gifts—and to receive them. Gifts are given on birthdays and on name days, on holidays such as International Women's Day (see Point 11, "Celebrations and Holidays"), on New Year's Day, for the birth of a child, and graduations. Wedding and housewarming presents are usually the most generous.

The most popular gift is flowers, but Russians also give and like to receive a box of chocolates, a cake, a bottle of wine, books, especially literature and illustrated art books, records, audio and video cassettes (both blank and recorded), jewelry, clothing (tee shirts, sweaters), shoes (especially sports shoes), electronic products, musical instruments, toys, and watches. More often than in the West, presents tend to be practical because of the difficult economic conditions in much of Russia. Practical gifts are especially popular for weddings and housewarmings. Although there are exceptions, one large gift will be presented, as opposed to several smaller ones.

Foreign visitors who are invited to a Russian house will always delight a hostess by presenting her with flowers as well as with books, liquor, candy, cosmetics, fancy soaps, items embellished with a school, company, city, or state logo, or toys if there are children in the house. Russians invariably bring a small gift (a toy, pen, crayon, or notebook) when visiting a house with a child. The gift should be offered immediately upon arrival.

Presents in Russia may be gift-wrapped or not, and there is no tradition that necessitates opening the gift in the giver's presence. Some Russians feel that opening a gift immediately is a sign of inappropriate eagerness; moreover, this action may embarrass those who did not bring a gift. If immediately opened, visitors may be surprised by a lack of gushing thanks for their gift and, if the gift is not opened upon receipt, no thanks may ever be received. Likewise, when gifts are brought to be given, say, to grandchildren or grandparents, there may never be an acknowledgment from the recipient, leaving the gift-giver to wonder whether the gifts were ever given in his or her name or passed off as someone else's!

❀

# 28. GREETINGS, SALUTATIONS, AND LEAVETAKINGS

In place of the ubiquitous American "hello," Russians have about five expressions that are appropriate at different times. "Z*drav*stvuyte"/**здра́вствуйте** can be used at any time of the day. So can the expression "pri*vet*"/**привéт**, when addressing close acquaintances (those on an even social level with the person offering the greeting). Greetings related to a particular time of the day are "*dob*roe *ut*ro," good morning (**дóброе у́тро**), "*do*briy den," good day (**дóбрый день**), and "*do*briy *ve*cher," good evening (**дóбрый вéчер**). They can be said to anyone, i.e., close friends as well as superiors.

In the United States we tend to say "hello" to people even upon a second or third encounter within the same day. Russians, however, will merely nod their head, or smile, or say "pri*vet*"/**привéт**. They will not repeat the word "*zdrav*stvuyte"/**здрáвствуйте** unless in frequent contact with foreign visitors.

After greeting someone, Russians frequently shake hands, and ask how you are doing. Most frequently this will be expressed by: "Kak de*la*"/**Как делá**? The English equivalent is "How are you?" In American culture the answer is frequently ignored, because the question is considered to be a greeting that does not require an answer. However, Russians expect an answer to this question. The most frequent answers from a Russian will be "nor*mal*no"/**норма́льно** or "niche*vo*"/**ничего́**, which literally mean "normal," and "nothing,"—best translated as "not too bad." Knowing that the answer will be one of these two words, some Russians greet each other by asking "How is your 'normal' (or 'nothing') doing?"

When leaving someone, "do sv*i*daniya," until we meet again (**до свида́ния**), is the most frequently used farewell. Young people and friends will use the term "po*ka*," so long (**пока́**), "vse*vo* khoro-shevo"/**всего́ хоро́шего**, "vse*vo* *do*brovo"/**всего́ до́брого** (all the best), or, very informally, simply "*do*brovo," literally "good" (**до́брого**). However, if the period of separation will be long, only "do sv*i*daniya"/**до свида́ния** is appropriate. If one does not expect to see a person again during one's lifetime, "farewell," "pro*shchay*te"/**проща́йте** is said. It literally means "forgive me." "Spo*koi*noy *no*chi"/**споко́йной но́чи** is used to say goodnight to someone getting ready to go to bed.

Russians and Americans differ in the way they leave a social gathering before it has ended. The Americans leave trying not to call attention to their early departure. Russians have a term for this: "ukho*dit* po-ameri*kan*ski"/**уходи́ть по-америка́нски**—to leave like an American. Others say "ukho*dit* po-an*gli*ski"/**уходи́ть по-англи́йски**—to leave like an Englishman. A Russian, in contrast, will acknowledge that an early departure is taking place. Likewise, when tardy for a class, Russian students will excuse themselves upon entering the classroom, whereas American students more likely will enter, trying not to call attention to themselves.

❀

# 29. GULAG (PRISON, EXILE), THE SECRET POLICE, AND THE KGB

The state security system, or the modern-day KGB, was instituted in the sixteenth century by Tsar Ivan the Terrible. In his struggles with the boyars (prominent members of the nobility), Ivan created the "oprichniki," who could destroy or exile a whole family. This police force, known as the "secret police" or the "third section," continued throughout the tsarist period. Those who ran afoul of the government could be executed, exiled, or sent to forced labor camps, "*ka*torga"/**ка́торга**, followed by a period of exile or "*ssi*lka"/**ссы́лка** from the capital. Fyodor Dostoevsky, considered—along with Leo Tolstoy—to be the foremost Russian writer of the nineteenth century, was arrested in 1849 for belonging to a radical political group. He spent four years in a labor camp, followed by six years in exile in the provinces, before being allowed to return to St. Petersburg (then the capital of Russia).

After the Bolshevik Revolution, the new leaders needed a state organization to suppress those opposed to the ideals of the Bolsheviks. "Kto ne s *na*mi, tot *pro*tiv nas." "Whoever is not with us is against us." («**Кто не с на́ми, тот про́тив нас.**»). The organization formed for that purpose was first known as Cheka from the letters of "Chrezvi*chai*naya Ko*mis*siya," Extraordinary Commission (**Чрезвыча́йная Коми́ссия**), a short form of its full title. After several changes of name and structure, it was named KGB in 1965, from the first letters of "Komi*tet* gosu*dar*stvennoy bezo*pa*snosti," Committee for State Security (**Комите́т госуда́рственной безопа́сности**). Its members, even today known as "che*ki*sti"/**чеки́сты**, were professionally respected, as those who had worked for the tsarist secret police had been. In 1991 their numbers were said to be about six million. They were aided and abetted by millions of informers, who either willingly or as a result of threats informed on the rest of the population—hence the distrust of anyone but one's closest friends or family members, the distrust of the telephone, the fear of public denunciations, and until recently the unwillingness to have anything to do with foreigners.

Those judged to be enemies of the people by the secret police under Communism in the early years after the Bolshevik Revolution included former aristocrats and tsarist army officers, and then later, rich peasants ("kulaks"); members of the intelligentsia, or anyone who stood in the way of Stalin as he consolidated power after Lenin's death. The years 1936 and 1937, known as the years of "the purges" or the "Great Terror," are especially notorious for the number of arrests and executions carried out by the secret police. Those not executed were sent to concentration camps to labor in the building of canals, power stations, and factories or to work in mines—all under the harshest of conditions.

After Stalin's death in 1953, the KGB (known then as MVD) became somewhat less active. Premier Nikita Khrushchev, in a closed session to the Twentieth Party Congress on February 20, 1956, delivered what has become known as "the secret speech" or the "de-Stalinization speech," in which he described the mass terror exercised by the KGB against the Soviet peoples. Rehabilitated former prisoners began to appear in society with tales of horror. Literary works written "for the drawer" began to circulate in unofficial samizdat editions, and some of these works were eventually published before Khrushchev was ousted from power. Anna Akhmatova's poem *Requiem*, written during the years of 1935–1940, related her own personal anguish, as she stood in endless lines attempting to determine the fate of her arrested son. The work was not published in Russia until the late 1980s, after the advent of Gorbachev's glasnost.

The work of author Aleksandr Solzhenitsyn, however, is most associated with this period in Russian history. Solzhenitsyn was arrested in 1945 after counterintelligence agents read a letter written by him to a friend, in which he obliquely disparaged Stalin. He was imprisoned for eight years. His experiences in prison provided Solzhenitsyn with the material for his novels. *One Day in the Life of Ivan Denisovich* appeared in 1962, after Khrushchev's intervention. For over two decades it was the major source of information about concentration camp experience.

With Khrushchev's ouster the brief literary thaw came to an end. Authors including Solzhenitsyn again wrote "for the drawer." Two of his later works, *Cancer Ward* and *The First Circle*, were forerunners to the monumental work that gave the whole prison experience its title, *The Gulag Archipelago*—a survey of the Soviet system of forced labor, using the author's own reminiscences and other documentary evidence. The word "gulag" comes from the Russian for Main Administration of Prisons, "*Glavnoye upravlenie lagerey*"/**Гла́вное управле́ние лагере́й**. Solzhenitsyn's last three works were refused publication in Russia and were published instead in the West. The appearance of the first volume of *The Gulag Archipelago* in Paris in 1973 caused an uproar in the Soviet Union and led to Solzhenitsyn's arrest and deportation.

In 1991 the KGB was replaced by the "Minis*ter*stvo bezo*pas*nosti," Russian Security Ministry (**Министе́рство безопа́сности**), which in turn was replaced in 1993 by the FSB, "Fede*ral*naya *sluzh*ba bezo*pas*nosti," Federal Security Service (**Федера́льная слу́жба безопа́сности**).

Vladimir Putin, who was elected president of Russia in 2000, had made his career in the secret services (specifically, the infamous KGB). At the end of the 1990s he headed FSB.

Every Soviet family suffered in some way during the years of Stalin's terror; millions were affected. Nevertheless, Stalin's crimes are not talked about that much in Russia today. Some people— especially those who believe in the need for a "strong man" (see Point 62) to lead Russia—even think that what happened was appropriate.

❁

## 30. HEALTH CARE

The Russian health care system is in a somewhat uncertain state at present. Until 1987 the state system predominated. All medical care (except for prescription drugs bought at pharmacies) was free. Although on occasion excellent medical care was administered, there were many inadequacies in the system, such as inadequate medical equipment and scarcity of prescription drugs. After 1987, the first medical co-ops emerged. Now the number of medical institutions that charge for their services is increasing. In addition, even within free medical institutions, some services are not free. In the 1990s, in order to improve medical care, various insurance systems were being examined.

The main illnesses that beset Russians are the common cold and the flu. The latter frequently sweeps a city as an epidemic. Although Russians believe that viruses spread colds, both doctors and patients believe that drafts, cold drinks, or sitting on cold surfaces such as floors or benches are also significant causes of colds. Russians who have a cold will not drink anything out of the refrigerator.

In 1990 the death rate surpassed the birth rate. In 1999 Russia's death rate was 14.7 people per 1000; the birth rate was 8.4 per 1000. That same year overall life expectancy fell one year to 65.5 years. Women lived an average 72 years, men 59.8. The leading cause of death is cardiovascular disease, followed by cancer. The "third disease," as it is frequently referred to in Russia, is alcoholism. Smoking also contributes to the worsening life expectancy figure.

With one exception there is no restriction on how many days a Russian may be sick and absent from work. The one exception is if a Russian is sick for four to six consecutive months. Then he or she is expected to obtain a "*vre*mennaya inva*lid*nost," temporary disability (**вре́менная инвали́дность**). Since the worker on medical leave does not receive a regular salary but a reduced one similar to a pension, most people try to avoid this status. They return to work for a while and then take off again, thus continuing to draw a regular salary.

The health-consciousness of Americans who watch their fat intake and routinely check their cholesterol count has not spread to Russia. Salt consumption is a less serious problem, because Russian food tends to be more bland than spicy. Checks for diabetes do take place.

Most foreigners who visit Russia comment on the extensive smoking in public places. The idea of "nonsmoking areas" has not yet reached Russia.

❁

## 31. HOUSING AND HOUSES

The bigger cities of Russia look very similar. Except for the historical central areas, Russian cities and towns share a similar skyline: block after block of tall apartment buildings. World War II destroyed 89 percent of the housing in areas of Russia occupied by the German army. After the war, the Russian government made a colossal effort to replace destroyed houses, to raze housing with no modern conveniences, and to build new housing for citizens who wished to move to the cities. In the late 1990s,

73 percent of all Russians lived in cities, and one in fifteen Russians lived in Moscow, where 80 percent of Russia's wealth was located.

The Stalin era in Moscow is known for its seven "wedding cake" buildings (four government offices, a hotel, apartments, and Moscow State University). In the Khrushchev era (1953–1964), the buildings tended to be five-storied, since buildings with more than five stories were required to have an elevator. The size of these apartments was rather small, and the ceilings were low. The goal was to build as many such apartments as possible to help the population. The buildings were expected to be torn down in 20 years; most of them, however, are still standing today.

In the Brezhnev era (1964–1982), the buildings typically had 9 to 12 stories and extended an entire block. Later, 14 to 18 stories per building were common. Buildings are usually made of concrete, prefabricated, and assembled onsite. Colorfully painted balconies add diversity to the buildings and to the city. Russians who travel to Europe and the United States invariably comment on the number of one- and two-story buildings found in cities there. Ilf and Petrov, two Russian writers who visited the United States in 1935, gave their travel memoirs the title "*Odnoetazhnaya Amerika*," *One-Storied America* (**Одноэта́жная Аме́рика**).

Most Russians in cities live in apartments given to them at no cost, which, prior to the early 1960s, belonged to the government. Each person was limited to 10.8 square yards of living space. In the 1990s this allotment was increased to 14.4 square yards, and some professionals were allowed an extra space of up to 21.2 square yards. The rent was minimal. A family of four (husband, wife, and two children) would typically have a two-room apartment, consisting of one room that served as a living/dining/bedroom for the parents and another room for the children. In addition, there would be areas not included in the two-room count: an entry area of some sort, a kitchen, and a "two-part" bathroom. In one little room would be a basin and a bathtub or shower and in another little room, the toilet. After 1962, Russians could purchase apartments in cooperative housing units. The individual rooms were larger, and the "so many meters per person" rule was not strictly enforced. Since 1992, Russians living in such cities as Moscow and St. Petersburg could "privatize" their apartments, for a nominal fee. They could then will them as they chose or sell them, which was not previously possible. Some cooperative apartment complexes have a "caretaker," similar to the French concierge, to help with maintenance and security. Foreign visitors note that when there is no caretaker, the outsides and common inner areas of Russian apartment houses frequently can be very poorly maintained. The insides of apartments, however, are a different matter—warm and cozy and attractively furnished. Repairs, such as those for heating and plumbing problems, are handled by a network of governmental offices, with some incurring charges, others not.

Some Russians live in communal housing. They have their own rooms, but all food preparation is done in one big kitchen. (The food is eaten in one's own apartment.) One or two bathrooms are shared by everyone. Individual meters (to measure water and electricity usage) for each family line the walls of the kitchen and the bathroom(s). Such housing is called "kommu*nal*ka"/**коммуна́лка**, from "kommu*nal*naya kvar*tira*," communal apartment (**коммуна́льная кварти́ра**).

Since the advent of perestroika, the influx of foreign businesses and their staffs have placed a premium on centrally located apartments. They are purchased by budding Russian capitalists, remodeled, and rented or sold to foreigners for offices or living quarters. The price for renting such an apartment can range from $700 to $3000 monthly for slightly less than nine square feet. If the buildings are centrally located and facing a street, their remodeled outside has to maintain the historic architecture of the area. New buildings, constructed inside courtyards, however, can be built in modern style, as can those in the suburbs. In Moscow, the Kuznetso region boasts a number of attractive luxury apartments/condominiums; in magazine ads for them the proprietors offer elite living quarters "for those who desire European quality and European style." To purchase a luxury condominium in such a high-rise building, one can expect to pay $1200 to $1500 per square meter. For example, a three-room condominium that measures 200 square meters (approximately 650 square feet) costs $270,000. The "new Russians" can afford such housing; ordinary Russians cannot.

Upon entering an apartment or a dacha, a Russian will immediately remove his or her shoes or boots and put on "*ta*pochki," slippers (тáпочки), which are conveniently located near the entrance. When visiting others in informal situations, guests will be offered slippers by hosts. Although at formal events guests will wear their own shoes, they will wipe them carefully before entering an apartment.

The cold weather in much of Russia (see Point 67, "Temperature") and the warmth that Russians crave for their apartments have influenced the construction of buildings. Windows typically are doubled windows to keep out the cold more effectively. However, for purposes of ventilation, a small hinged windowpane, which can be opened separately from the window, is installed in the top part of the window. This "*for*tochka"/ **фóрточка** has been used by many a visitor to counter the heat in Russian apartments. (See Point 61, "Street Names and Addresses" on how to find an address and enter a building.)

❁

## 32. HYGIENE

Like many Europeans, Russians do not consider it essential to take daily showers or baths. Before the advent of bathrooms, the weekly trip to the banya (See Point 8, "Banya") served as the means to cleanliness, and a weekly bath is still not uncommon. This fact, plus a reluctance to dry-clean or wash clothes (washing machines in Russian homes are still not common, and those that do exist are semiautomatic), often can lead to "fragrant" encounters. However, in recent years attitudes toward hygiene are changing. Deodorants are becoming more readily available and used. No matter how frequently Russians take a shower or bath, it is generally done prior to retiring for the night. Many Russians are most perplexed by the habit of daily washing of hair; some Russian doctors consider washing hair more than once a week bad for the hair.

❁

# 33. ICE AND THE PURITY OF RUSSIAN WATER

As is true in much of Europe, Russians do not use ice cubes in their drinks. With the exception of vodka, beer, and champagne, drinks are generally offered at room temperature and without ice. Russians with a sore throat or sick with the flu will never drink anything refrigerated, much less anything that has an ice cube in it. Today ice is available in hotels that cater to tourists. But should it be used? There are Russian ecologists who consider one-fourth of Russia's drinking water unsafe. The city of St. Petersburg, built on a swamp in the early eighteenth century, is well-known for its brownish-looking water, beset with the parasite *Giardia lamblia*. One should not drink this water under any circumstances, but rather rely on bottled water. And remember, if water is to be avoided in a particular locality, so should ice.

✿

# 34. THE INTELLIGENTSIA

In the nineteenth century, the term *intelligentsia* referred to educated people who generally held radical left-wing views and acted on their consciences by criticizing the existing Russian order. Idealism characterized the intelligentsia. After the emancipation of the serfs in 1861, many members of the intelligentsia joined a group that came to be known as the Populists and went into the countryside to educate the freed serfs. After the revolution of 1917, the intelligentsia was considered unreliable and was discriminated against by the Bolsheviks; good jobs, admission to colleges, and memberships in the Communist Party were hard to obtain.

In the 1930s the Communist Party strove to create a new, loyal intelligentsia. In 1936 Stalin proclaimed that the intelligentsia was a stratum of society, "pros*loy*ka"/**просло́йка** [not a class], and that students, independent professional people, and nonmanual employees above the clerical level belonged to it. The intelligentsia was courted. Stalin labeled writers "the engineers of human souls." Writers, artists, and composers who joined professional associations received privileges such as passes or "pu*tyov*ki"/**путёвки** for stays at a "Dom *tvor*chestva," House of Creativity (**Дом творчества**), where they could work or vacation. The values of the intelligentsia were praised and the arts were subsidized.

With the demise of the Soviet Union, the intelligentsia became impoverished. The monetary support offered by the government to artistic endeavors largely vanished. As a result, many cultural undertakings ended. For example, subsidized journals such as *Soviet Film* ceased publication. The Western orientation of the arts and the new market economy hurt Russian artistic efforts. Businessmen took over the Houses of Creativity; they could afford to stay there, by and large the intelligentsia could not. Many members of the intelligentsia left Russia for temporary jobs in the West or emigrated. Many of those who remain are eager to take advantage of the new freedoms to do creative work in their professions. (See Point 71, "Tsereteli, Zurab Konstantinovich.")

❀

# 35. INTRODUCTIONS

Upon being introduced to a Russian, one usually shakes hands. In American culture in a social or business setting, it is considered important that introductions be made to people who are not acquainted with one another. This is not the case in Russia. You may enter a room where two people are seated, only one of whom you know. That person may make no effort to introduce you to the unknown one, while entering into a warm conversation with you. Or you may be in a social or a business setting with acquaintances when someone unknown joins you, and no attempt is made to introduce that person. Your choice is to take the initiative and introduce yourself (in the first and second examples), or, in the second example, to remain silent.

It is unclear why Russians are not more forthcoming with introductions. When queried, they refer to lack of proper upbringing. However, the suspicion and false denunciations heard of or experienced, especially during Stalin's reign, when only the nearest and dearest were trusted and unknown people were avoided, may remain in the Russian psyche. If a foreign visitor lets one's Russian friends know that he or she likes introductions to take place, the friends usually graciously comply and remember this fact in the future.

❀

## 36. IN THE KITCHEN

Just as in American homes, the kitchen seems to be the most popular room in Russian homes. Family members and close friends gather there to eat and chat. If you are invited into the kitchen for a meal, a cup of tea, or something stronger, consider it a compliment. It is in the kitchen that the most meaningful conversations take place between a visitor and a Russian. Russian love for discussion lasting long into the night is well-known. A visitor who has an opportunity to participate in this Russian experience is a lucky one indeed. Such opportunities are to be especially treasured in Russia's new capitalist era. The pace of life has speeded up, leaving less time for leisurely lingering in the kitchen.

The table in a small Russian kitchen is generally surrounded by stools, which are pushed under the table when not in use. By the sink is a place where dishes can dry after being washed. The shelf just above the sink is similarly intended for this purpose. The bottom shelf does not have a solid plank but slots, so that dishes placed above it in a dish "caddy" can drip dry. Dishwashing liquid may be used, or, a dishcloth or a sponge is run across a bar of soap. Dishwashers are very rare. The gas stove has an oven and four burners ignited by a match or an electrical starter. Some families have two refrigerators and a freezer, sometimes located in a corridor. The extra refrigerator and the freezer are especially important for those who have a dacha and need a place to store pickled vegetables, preserves, and the meat of animals raised in the country. Russians frequently put food left over in a pot directly into the refrigerator. Often no cover is placed on the pot.

❁

# 37. LETTERS, GREETING CARDS, AND ANNOUNCEMENTS

Letter-writing is more prevalent in Russia than in the West. Distrust of the telephone may account partly for this fact. (See Point 65, "The Telephone.")

Envelopes in Russia are addressed in reverse order to those in the United States:[1]

| | | |
|---|---|---|
| postal code (index) | 121433 | **1214333** |
| city and city region | Mosk*v*a | **Москва́** |
| street name | P*e*rviy Akade*m*icheski proe*z*d | **Пе́рвый Академи́ческий прое́зд** |
| building and apartment numbers | Dom 34/4, kv. 107 | **дом 34/4, кв. 107** |
| addressee (in the dative case) | Ev*d*okhinoy, *Li*lii Petro*v*ne | **Евдо́хиной Ли́лии Петро́вне** |

Care must be exercised as to where the "To" and "From" information is written. Many of these envelopes come already preprinted with the words "ku*da*," where (**куда́**), and "ko*mu*," to whom (**кому́**). There

---

[1]Stress on Russian words is indicated here, as elsewhere in this book. However, Russians do not write stress marks in written Russian.

is a special place on the envelope for the postal code; in order for sorting machines to read the numbers, they are written following a specific style illustrated on the envelope. When the envelopes are not preprinted, the "To" address is written one-quarter of the distance from the top and the left of the envelope. The "From" address is then written at the bottom quarter of the envelope. A thick black line separates the "To" and "From" parts of the envelope.

Visitors from Russia staying in the United States and writing letters to Russia should be warned to write their own address in the upper left corner of the envelope and the address of the person to whom they are writing in the lower right quandrant of the envelope. Many visitors have had their letters returned because their own addresses had been written in the place where Americans address their correspondence.

Centered on the right in personal letters one writes the address (optional) and date, and in official letters, the address and date.

## Personal letters

Salutations in personal letters are centered on the first line of the letter after the (optional) address and date and generally end with an exclamation point:

| | | |
|---|---|---|
| Dorog*oy* (mo*y*) . . . , | (My) dear . . . [masculine] | дорого́й (мой) . . . , |
| Dorog*aya* (mo*ya*) . . . , | (My) dear . . . [feminine] | дорога́я (моя́) . . . , |
| Dorog*ie* (mo*i*) . . . , | (My) dear . . . [plural] | дороги́е (мои́) . . . , |
| Rod*noy* (*nash*) | (Our) own . . . [masculine] | Родно́й (наш) . . . |
| Rod*naya* (*nas*ha) | (Our) own . . . [feminine] | Родна́я (на́ша) . . . |
| Rod*nie* (*nas*hi) | (Our) own . . . [plural] | Родны́е (на́ши) . . . |
| *Zdra*vstvuyte, (mo*i*) *mi*liye! | Greetings (my) dear ones! | Здра́вствуйте, (мои́) ми́лые! |
| Priv*et* iz Chik*ago*! | Hello from Chicago! | Приве́т из Чика́го! |

47

It is considered rude to begin a letter with the name of a person, i.e., "Marina!" without an endearing term in front of it, i.e., "Dear Marina."

Paragraphs are always indented ("*kras*naya stro*ka*"/**кра́сная строка́**) in Russian letters. Block style is not used.

## Closings in personal letters

| | | |
|---|---|---|
| S lyu*bov*yu, | With love, | **С любо́вью,** |
| Do svi*da*niya/<br>  Do *vstre*chi, | Goodbye/Until<br>  we meet again, | **До свида́ния/**<br>  **До встре́чи.** |
| Tse*lu*yu/<br>  Obni*ma*yu, | I kiss you<br>  (Kisses. . . )/<br>  I embrace you, | **Целу́ю/Обнима́ю,** |
| Vse*vo* khoroshevo/<br>  *do*brovo! | All the best! | **Всего́ хоро́шего/**<br>  **до́брого!** |
| Zhe*la*yu u*da*chi. | I wish you success. | **Жела́ю уда́чи.** |
| Zhdu ot*ve*ta. | I await (your)<br>  answer. | **Жду отве́та.** |

## Business and other formal letters

Salutations in business and other formal letters are centered (as in personal letters) on the first line after the address and date and end in an exclamation point. Typical salutations are:

| | | |
|---|---|---|
| Uvazha*em*-iy, -aya,<br>  -ie | Respected | **Уважа́ем-ый, -ая,**<br>  **-ые** |
| Mnogouva*zha*emiy,<br>  -aya, -ie | Much respected | **Многоуважа́ем-ый,**<br>  **-ая, -ые** |
| Glubokouva*zha*emiy,<br>  -aya, -ie . . . , | Deeply respected<br>  [masculine, feminine,<br>  plural endings] . . . , | **Глубокоуважа́ем-ый**<br>  **-ая, -ые . . . ,** |
| Gospo*din*, gospo*zha*,<br>  gospo*da* . . . , | Mr., Miss or Mrs.,<br>  Sirs . . . , | **Господи́н, госпожа́,**<br>  **господа́ . . . ,** |

It is considered more polite to put an adjective such as "Respected" in front of "Mr.," rather than starting out a letter only with the latter.

| | | |
|---|---|---|
| S uva*zhy*eniem, | Respectfully, | **С уваже́нием** |
| *I*skrenne, | Sincerely, | **И́скренне,** |
| Zaranee | In advance I | **Зара́нее** |
| b1ago*da*ren, | [masculine, | **благода́рен,** |
| blago*da*rna, | feminine, | **благода́рна,** |
| blago*da*rni | plural | **благода́рны,** |
| | adjectival | |
| | endings] | |
| | thank you, | |
| Zaranee | In advance I | **Зара́нее** |
| blago*daryu*, | thank you, | **благодарю́** |
| | [verb form] | |

Greeting cards are popular in Russia. People send cards to note birthdays, name days, wedding anniversaries, and major holidays. New Year's Eve, International Women's Day, and Victory Day are the most popular occasions for sending cards. May Day cards and November 7th cards in particular have lost their importance since the 1990s, while Christmas and Easter cards have become increasingly popular. In addition there are cards to commemorate a baby's birth, a first paycheck, and for a housewarming. And just as we in the United States have our "Secretary's Day," Russians have "Builders' Day," "Teachers' Day," "Day Dedicated to the Medical Profession," and so forth.

❀

# 38. MEALS AND MEALTIMES

The Russian day starts with a "*za*vtrak," breakfast (**за́втрак**), in the morning, "*obed*," dinner (**обе́д**), around 1:00—the main meal of the day, with appetizers, soup, a main dish, and a dessert—and "*uz*hin," supper (**у́жин**), around 7:00 PM or later, with appetizers, a main course, and possibly dessert. The concept of "lunch" is generally unknown in Russia, although lately because of a large number of foreign visitors, the word is being heard and understood as something in between a breakfast and a Russian dinner. A "*pold*nik," afternoon snack (**по́лдник**), around 4:00 PM, is popular with the children (after their naps) both at home and at school, as well as with adults in sanatoriums and rest houses.

At breakfast, eggs, sausage, cold cuts, kasha, hot dogs, cheese, bread with butter, and tea or coffee are served. Hot cereals, especially oatmeal, are popular with mothers feeding school-age children. Since the 1990s, cold cereals produced in Russia or imported from abroad have also been available.

"*Zaku*ski," appetizers (**заку́ски**), begin dinner, the main meal of the day. Frequently, they are the most interesting part of the dinner: caviar, pâté, pickles, cheese, smoked fish, herring, all kinds of mushrooms, marinated vegetables, and various kinds of "salads"— consisting of vegetables, potatoes, eggs, meat, or fish. It is easy to mistake the appetizers for the main meal. (It might be wise, if it can be done politely, to inquire what is on the menu at the start of the meal.) "*Per*voe"/**Пе́рвое** is a soup course, while "vto*roe*"/**второ́е** includes meat or fish dishes, with an accompaniment of potatoes, rice or noodles, and fresh (when available) or marinated vegetables. "*Trete*"/**Тре́тье** is a dessert course, possibly including chocolates, cakes, and dishes such as "kom*pot*," stewed fruit (**компо́т**), or "ki*sel*," a type of fruit purée (**кисе́ль**).

The evening meal is a version of dinner without a soup course and sometimes without a dessert course. However, in the countryside, where workers in the fields do not have soup with their noon meal, soup is eaten at the evening meal.

Tea is the most frequently served breakfast drink even for children. Drinking orange juice or the like is not a Russian tradition in the mornings. Mineral water or soft drinks may be offered during dinner and supper, and they will most likely be served at room temperature, as Russians generally do not use ice. For festive occasions, bottles of champagne, wine, vodka, or cognac may also be on the table. Tea or coffee, if available, will be offered at the end of the meal. (See Points 33, "Ice and the Purity of Russian Water," 64, "Tea," and 75, "Vodka and Drinking.")

Russian cooking is one of the distinctive cuisines of the world, and the Russian table in a family setting is a feast for the eyes as well as the palate. Its most famous dishes are "ik*ra*," caviar (**икра́**), sturgeon's eggs (if black) or salmon eggs (if red), served with bread, pancakes, or potatoes; a beet-based soup, "borshch" (**борщ**), which orginated in Ukraine; and a beef, mushroom, and sour cream sauce dish, beef stroganoff ("bef-*strog*anov"/**беф-стро́ганов**), created by a French chef for the Russian Count Stroganov. Russian pancakes, called "bli*ni*"/**блины́**, have saved many a working Russian hostess faced with unexpected guests and a bare cupboard. Pancakes, served with caviar or herring, sour cream, and jams, and accompanied by vodka, delight many a foreign visitor, as recounted by opera singer Galina Vishnevskaya (wife of the cellist and conductor Mstislav Rostropovich), before the couple was expelled from the former Soviet Union. (See Points 4, "At the Table," and 51, "Restaurants.")

❀

# 39. MILESTONES

A newborn Russian baby is unlikely to be baptized. In the late 1980s only one-third of the Soviet population were believers in God, and half of those were Moslems. However, a baby born into a Russian Orthodox family is baptized within three months or so of birth by being immersed in water.

In all likelihood, except for the very rich, both parents work, so a child is generally placed in a nursery or childcare center. Russian youngsters enter first grade at age 6 or 7. At age 14 a Russian receives an internal passport, indicating place of residence and including a photograph. Prior to 1997, a Russian received this passport at age 16, and his or her nationality was also indicated. However, full citizenship rights, including the right to vote, obtain a driver's license, and get married, are not granted until age 18. Graduation from high school, generally at 17 years of age, is marked by celebrating all night.

A Russian must be 18 to marry. On receipt of special permission, girls may marry earlier than boys. Russians celebrate birthdays not in a restaurant or at dinner at a friend's house but by staying at home in the evening on their birthdays while relatives and friends drop by with congratulations. The person celebrating the birthday provides the food, not the guests. Likewise, should a celebration take place during the day in the workplace, the "birthday person" provides the food for the gathering. Gifts, however, are presented in the name of the work group to the celebrant.

Upon reaching the age of 18, all males are required to serve in the Russian military for two years. University students may receive a deferment.

Retirement age for a woman is 55 provided she has a 20-year record of work service, or "stazh"/**стаж**. Males retire at age 60, with 25 years of work service. When infirmity or serious ill health comes, only if there are no living children will a Russian retire to a nursing home, "dom dlya prestarelikh"/**дом для престаре́лых**. Nursing homes are rare; the ones that exist are largely sponsored by organizations such as professional trade unions. The reputation of nursing homes is not very favorable.

When someone passes away, family and friends gather to bid farewell. This can take place at home or in the workplace. Frequently the gathering will be at the cemetery, where the body will be in an open casket. In Russian Orthodox families, the body lies in an open casket at home for one to three nights; friends come to say farewell and prayers are said. The deceased may also be taken to the church, and a special funeral service, "otpevanie"/**отпева́ние**, accompanied by a choir, may take place.

There are no funeral homes of the kind we have in the United States, but funeral services do exist that help the bereaved cope. If the deceased is not to be laid out at home, they arrange for a viewing site, set up visiting hours for family and friends, and on the day of the funeral, provide a funeral bus to transport the body and those accompanying the deceased (who sit on the sides of the bus) to the place of burial or cremation. Because of lack of cemetery space in large cities, cremations are more frequent at present. On the day of the burial, farewell words are said, then the body in a casket is lowered into the ground. Each person throws a handful of earth into the grave. The funeral bus will then take family and guests, generally to a private home, but occasionally to a private room at a restaurant, to observe a wake, "po*minki*"/**поми́нки**. Two dishes that will definitely grace the table are pancakes, "bli*ni*"/**блины́**, and "ku*tya*"/**кутья́**—a thick, steamed dish of rice or wheat with raisins, honey, and nuts. While words of affection for the deceased are said over drinks, they are not considered "toasts," and glasses are not clinked, because clinking is associated with joyful events and is inappropriate when someone has died.

If the body is laid out at home, by tradition, all the mirrors in the home of the deceased are covered until the ninth day, "*devyatiy* den"/**девя́тый день**, after the death, at which time tradition says that the soul of the deceased departs the earth. Friends and family gather at this time, and there is eating and drinking. Forty days, "soroko*voy* den"/**сороково́й день**, after the death, family and friends again gather, visit the cemetery, and again share a rich table. One year after the death, family and close friends gather yet one more time. Although there may be variations, generally the meal begins with pancakes that are drizzled with honey and then eaten rolled up. If flowers are brought to any of these occasions, they need to be in even numbers in accordance with custom.

Before 1991, milestones connected with the Communist Party included admittance to "oktya*brya*ta"/**октября́та** (the Octobrists—from the month the 1917 Bolshevik Revolution took place) for youngsters ages 6 to 9, then to "pio*nery*"/**пионе́ры** (the Pioneers), for those ages 10 to 15, and then on to "komso*mol*tsi"/**комсомо́льцы** (the Komsomols, or Young Communists), for those ages 14 to 28. These organizations were disbanded in 1991. Before 1991 acceptance into the Communist Party was considered to be a great honor and an occasion to celebrate; at that time 7 to 10 percent of the population were members of the Communist Party. In 1991 there were 19 million members of the Communist Party in what was then the Soviet Union.

## 40. MONETARY UNITS

The main monetary units of Russia are the ruble (or rouble), "rubl"/**рубль** and the kopeck, "ko*pey*ka"/**копéйка**, with one hunded kopecks equal to one ruble, just as one hundred cents make a dollar. One-, 5-, 10-, and 50-kopeck coins exist. However, since the inflation of the 1990s, generally only the 10- and 50-kopeck coins are used. The costs of goods have risen steadily. The cost of a metro ride, which in 1990 was five kopecks, rose to 250 kopecks in 1992, and in 2000 to 5 rubles (500 kopecks).

All kopecks and rubles minted or printed before 1998 are worthless and hence not in circulation. (In contrast, the older stamps can be used, with a subtraction of the last three digits. Thus, a 5000-ruble stamp now is a 5-ruble stamp and can be used.)

❀

## 41. MUSHROOMS

In late summer and early fall there is no more popular sport in Russia than "gathering mushrooms" ("sobi*rat* gri*bi*"/**собирáть грибы́**). Russians head for the woods loaded with empty baskets. From childhood they have accompanied their parents on such outings and have become thoroughly acquainted with where mushrooms are to be found and which mushrooms are edible, though poisonings do occur from time to time. In the evening, people with loaded baskets return to the villages or board trains back to the big cities. Food gathered in such a manner is a help with the food budget. Mushrooms that are not immediately enjoyed are preserved for later consumption. Pickled, marinated mushrooms appear at the table on festive occasions during the rest of the year. Russians do not eat mushrooms raw and are surprised to find raw mushrooms in tossed salads or with an appetizer dip.

❀

## 42. NEKUL*TURNO*, UNCULTURED (*НЕКУЛЬТУ́РНО*)

Countries and cultures have standards that they consider a minimum for behavior. Those who violate these standards are labeled "uncultured." The Soviet Union had a set list of actions that were considered unacceptable. (In the mid 1990s attitudes were changing slightly on the do's and don'ts of behavior.) Some examples of unacceptable behavior: not checking one's coat in the cloakroom (it is not permitted to take it into a theater or a restaurant), sitting on the floor in public buildings, putting one's feet on a chair in front of one, or for a man, sitting with one's legs sprawled out. Such actions frequently elicited the admonition "one may not/one should not"—nel*zya*/**нельзя́**.

## 43. PATRONYMICS

Except within a family or among very close friends, Russians address each other by their first names "*i*mya"/**и́мя** (in full form, not a diminutive) and patronymics, or "*ot*chestvo"/**о́тчество**. When Russians are among foreign visitors this practice may be less prevalent.

To form a patronymic, a man adds the suffix "-ovich" ("-evich") [**-ович (-евич)**] to his father's first name I*van* + "-ovich" = I*van* I*van*ovich" (**Ива́н + -ович = Ива́н Ива́нович**), while a woman adds "-ovna" (-evna) [**-овна (-евна)**] to her father's first name I*van* + "-ovna" = "Mar*i*na I*van*ovna (**Ива́н + -овна = Мари́на Ива́новна**).

Occasionally, among relatively close friends, or when wishing to show respect to someone with whom one is very close, Russians will address a person with only the patronymic, i.e., without the first name.

# 44. PENSIONS

The switch to a cumulative pension system is just now being discussed in Russia, and at present pensions are being paid off from one pension fund, which is accumulated from obligatory payments made by all businesses and organizations. Various people receive pensions: the disabled, retired veterans, orphans. However, the majority are old-age pensioners: for women age 55, for men, 60. Women earn a minimum pension payment after working for at least 20 years, men, at least 25.

Due to the high inflation rate since 1991, pension payments have risen; however, the pensioners' real buying power has fallen significantly. An important goal of Russia's government in the late 1990s/early 2000s was to raise the minimum pension, and as a result the difference between the maximum pension (upon complete work history) and the minimum pension (society's help to those who had not worked at all) was diminished. For example, in Moscow, where the city's budget allows an extra federal pension and thus in some small manner compensates for the greater expense of living in the city, almost all the pensioners receive the same pension, namely 1100 rubles per month, or around $40, as of the year 2000. This sum is lower than the minimum living standard for Moscow, which is 3000 rubles, or around $110.

Government sector employees are in a more advantageous situation, especially if they are career civil servants or blue-collar laborers at government-run industries with long seniority. Their pension is 80 percent of their last salary, and many receive a pension that is many times higher than the maximum pension that nongovernmental workers receive. However, the wages paid by the government are lower than what the private sector pays, and arrears in pay are very common.

Government leaders hope that in the future they can raise pensions to the level of a living wage. However, Russia's unfavorable demographic situation (low birthrate and the growing proportion of retired and unemployed) makes this task difficult.

# 45. PEOPLE'S NAMES AND NAME DAYS

Some Russian first names have been popular for generations: there have always been many boys named "Vo*lo*dya" (**Воло́дя**), "Ilya," (**Илья́**), "Sa*sha*" (**Cáша**), "Mi*sha*" (**Ми́ша**), "An*drey* (**Андре́й**), and "Ser*yozha*" (**Серёжа**); many girls have been called "Ma*riya*" (**Мари́я**), "Na*tasha*" (**Ната́ша**),"Ga*lya*" (**Га́ля**), "Ta*tyana*" (**Татья́на**), or "A*nna*" (**А́нна**). From time to time, other names have become fashionable. In the early Soviet period, some children received newly coined names such as "Vladi*lena*" or "Ni*nel*" (**Владиле́на** or **Нине́л**)—to honor "Vla*dimir Le*nin" (**Влади́мир Ле́нин**)—the latter name is Lenin spelled backwards—or even "Elektrifi*katsiya*" (**Электрифика́ция**) or "Dneprog*es*" (**Днепрогэ́с**)—to show enthusiastic support for the goal of complete electrification of the country or the building of a hydroelectric station on the Dnieper. Foreign names have also been popular at times, especially in the late 1930s before World War II: "*Robert*" (**Ро́берт**), "Margarita" (**Маргари́та**), "Edu*ard*" (**Эдуа́рд**). In the 2000s popular Russian male names are "I*van*" (**Ива́н**), "Boris" (**Бори́с**), K*irill* (**Кири́лл**), and "D*mitriy*" (**Дми́трий**), while for girls the popular names are Yekate*rina* (**Екатери́на**), A*nn*a (**А́нна**), "Yeliza*veta*" (**Елизаве́та**), "*Darya*" (**Да́рья**), and "Anasta*siya*" (**Анастаси́я**).

The Russian word for "last name" is fa*miliya*/**фами́лия**, which must not be confused with the English word "family," "se*mya*"/**семья́** in Russian. Common last names are: "Kuznet*sov*" (**Кузнецо́в**), "Ivan*ov*" (**Ивано́в**), "Petrov" (**Петро́в**), "Si*dorov*" (**Си́доров**), "Smir*nov*" (**Смирно́в**), "Plot*nikov*" (**Пло́тников**), "Pav*lov*" (**Па́влов**), "Nikitin" (**Ники́тин**), and "Mi*khay*lov" (**Миха́йлов**). Frequently a last name is formed from a first name, e.g., "Ivan*ov*" (**Ивано́в**) from "Ivan" (**Ива́н**), or from a profession, e.g., "Kuznet*sov*" (**Кузнецо́в**), from (black) "smith."

The gender of first names in their formal form can be determined from their endings. Most female names end in -a/-**a** or -ya/-**я**. "Na*tasha*," "Ga*lya*" (**Ната́ша, Га́ля**); masculine names in a consonant, "I*van*," "Boris" (**Ива́н, Бори́с**). Female diminutives end in -a/-**a** and -ya/-**я**, "Ira,"

"*Ka*tya" (**Йра, Ка́тя**), and so do many male diminutives, "*Sasha*," "*Borya*" (**Са́ша, Бо́ря**). Masculine last names end in consonants, "Smir*nov*"/**Смирно́в**, feminine in -a/-**a** or -ya/-**я**, "Smir*nova*," "Kali-*nov*skaya" (**Смирно́ва, Калино́вская**), and the plural form of last names ends -y/-**ы**, -i/-**и**, or -iye/-**ие** "Smir*novy*," "Kali*nov*skie" (**Смирно́вы, Калино́вские**).

Those Russians who are Russian Orthodox or (less commonly) Roman Catholics generally have a first name chosen from an official list of saints' names. Each day of the year, one or more saints are honored by these churches. Their names appear on church calendars. When parents choose a name for a child, the day the church honors a saint by that name becomes the child's name day. Prior to the 1917 revolution, name days were celebrated more frequently with friends than were birthdays. From the calendar, everyone knew a friend's name day and would visit the friend on that day. The party for Tatyana in Aleksandr Pushkin's *Eugene Onegin* (and in Tchaikovsky's opera of the same name) is held on her name day, not on her birthday. Note that the party takes place at Tatyana'a mother's estate. For both name days and birthdays the celebrant acts as host to those who wish to drop by and celebrate the event.

❀

# 46. PHYSICAL DISTANCE AND CONTACT

As in other European countries such as Spain, Russians do not require the physical distance between two speakers that American culture demands. For them a distance of 12 inches is quite normal; hence while conversing a Russian is likely to stand closer to his or her speaking companion than an American. The same is true for people waiting in line, eating in a restaurant, or sitting on park benches. In crowded city transport, especially during rush hours, people are frequently packed like sardines, resulting in considerable unavoidable shoving and pushing. This situation does not lead to the flaring of tempers, though those boarding or exiting buses too slowly may get chastised for their slowness.

Russians have physical contact with each other in their daily lives more frequently than we do in the United States. On the street, girls, women, and couples may stroll arm in arm. People shake hands readily. Upon meeting an acquaintance, especially one they have not seen for a while, some Russian men are likely to embrace and kiss the person on the cheek (sometimes three times, alternating cheeks). Occasionally, the kiss may even be on the lips. There are many men, however, who limit their greetings to a handshake or a clap on the shoulder. Touching the person one is conversing with is also common, a sign of camaraderie. In the United States, by contrast, some consider such touching invasive.

Russians, like other Europeans, perceive distances differently than Americans do. When a Russian says that he or she lives near something, an American imagines a 5–10 minute walk. In reality, a 20–30 minute trek may be in order.

❁

# 47. POLITICS AND PARTIES

The 1917 Bolshevik Revolution brought the Communist Party to pre-eminence. Up until 1991 it was the only legal political party in the Soviet Union. Membership in the Communist Party was considered an honor and a privilege. Those desiring to join the Communist Party generally became members of the Komsomol (see Point 39, "Milestones"). They were expected to lead a life of commitment to party goals and service to society. Recommendations for membership and support from three current Communist Party members were required. Communist Party membership varied from 5 to 10 percent of the population.

Being a member of the Communist Party was a great help in one's career. Managers of factories, principals of high schools, and chairs of university departments, as well as people in higher positions, were all expected to be Party members. However, since the Communist Party was a party of the proletariat, care was always taken to assure that a significant portion of the members were workers.

Since there was only one party in the Soviet Union, elections consisted not of two people competing against each other, but of the population voting for *one name* on the ballot. That person had been nominated by the Communist Party committee and then presented as a candidate by trade unions and workers' organizations. Usually, members of these organizations had already earlier approved the nomination.

On the day of voting, the whole population was expected to participate in the elections. Volunteers checked to see who had not voted toward closing time and made rounds encouraging and cajoling the public to vote. Indeed, while the Communist Party was in power, at least according to official statistics, over 99% of the population voted.

Prior to Mikhail Gorbachev's time, the government and the Communist Party functioned as one. Gorbachev's perestroika in the mid-1980s brought to life a number of political organizations and movements (such as the Democratic Platform), which—although they did not dare to call themselves parties—created the foundation for the multiparty system that now exists in Russia. The first political alternative movements opposed the ruling Communist Party on two major issues: totalitarian Stalinist ideology and proletarian internationalism, as exemplified in the slogan "Proletarians of the World Unite!" By the end of the 1980s, Russia's major cities had "Popular Fronts," which integrated unofficial, pro-democratic, public groups and national–patriotic unions. Toward the end of the 1980s, Pamyat, a group within the All-Russian Society for the Preservation of Historical and Cultural Monuments, attracted public attention because of its anti-Semitic, nationalist orientation. After Chernobyl, ecologically and environmentally minded groups, known as Greens, began to campaign on issues such as pollution and the presence of nuclear power stations in municipal areas. Another group, Memorial, strove to rehabilitate the victims of Stalinism and to raise funds for a memorial in their honor.

It was in 1989 that the first contested elections in the Soviet Union in over 70 years took place. Gorbachev decided that the seats for the Congress of People's Deputies of the Soviet Union should have competing candidates. For the first time, ordinary citizens became politically involved. In the process, many challenged the Communist Party officials. The physicist Andrei Sakharov was one of the deputies elected; he played a significant role when the Congress convened in May 1989. A political transformation took place as factions mushroomed.

At the Twenty-Eighth Communist Party Congress in July, 1990, Gorbachev tried to maneuver between the right and left factions and satisfied neither. Toward the end of the Congress, Boris Yeltsin publicly announced his resignation from the Communist Party. This action was repeated the following day by St. Peterburg's (then Leningrad's) Mayor Anatoly Sobchak and Moscow's then Mayor Gavriil Popov. Other important leaders soon followed suit.

The failed coup of August 1991 against Gorbachev by the hard-liners signaled the end of the Communist Party as it had existed for over 75 years. The party split up into opposing factions which became separate parties. In December 1991 the Soviet Union was officially dissolved. Power passed to Boris Yeltsin. In June, 1991, he was the first person to run in nationwide elections for President of Russia. He won with 60 percent of the popular vote. The dramatic events of September-October 1993, when Yeltsin's forces overwhelmed his opponents at the Communist-dominated Parliament, led to a proliferation of political parties.

In 1994 there were over 60 poltical parties registered with the Ministry of Justice in Russia; in 1999 they numbered over 100. Parties, which some in the West would not call parties but voter blocs or political movements, are constantly changing; they mature, merge, split, or dissolve. Having no previous experience with a multiparty system, Russia is just learning how to deal with them. At this point, the parties are small and weak, and their allegiance is centered on a political leader more than a philosophy.

The parties can be divided into three groups and various subgroups. The three main groups may be called "democrats," "communists," and "nationalists." The latter two groups have similar philosophies and are joined in a Union of Patriotic Strength, "So*yuz* patrio*ti*cheskikh sil"/**Сою́з патриоти́ческих сил**. The communist-oriented parties want to see Russia become a superpower with a state-run, planned economy, following Marxist principles. Some desire the restoration of the Soviet Union, at least of its Slavic part. Some denounce the Bolshevik heritage. They invoke "socialism with a human face" and an economy that is largely state-dominated but with some small allowance for private enterprise.

Nationalist parties share a common view of Russia as a superpower, with Russians as the dominant ethnic group. They believe that Russia has its own unique destiny apart from the Western world. Their economic platforms, however, differ. Some advocate political pluralism and a mixed market economy, while others want ro bring back the monarchy, orthodoxy, and a state-run economy. Nationalist parties are often backed by paramilitary structures led by former "black berets" and Afghan war veterans. In the parliamentary elections of December 1993 the misnamed Liberal Democratic Party, with Vladimir Zhirinovsky at its head, received 23 percent of the vote. Zhirinovsky has proclaimed his desire to see Russia become a colonial power and to regain the former territories of the Russian tsarist empire, including Poland, Finland, the three Baltic States, and even Alaska. At the end of the 1990s, Zhirinovsky's popularity fell to one-fourth of its former level. In the 2000 elections, his party received only with difficulty the 5 percent vote essential for a party's deputies to enter the Duma.

There are about 30 democratically oriented parties. The most important of them, as represented in the Duma, are "*Ya*bloko"/**Я́блоко**; Fatherland—All Russia, "O*t*echestvo—Vsya Ro*ssiya*"/**Отéчество—Вся Росси́я**; and the Union of Right-Wing Forces, "So*yuz pra*vikh sil"/**Сою́з пра́вых сил**. These parties are pro-Western and in favor of a free-market economy (hence they are frequently called "*ri*nochniki"/**ры́ночники**, from the Russian word for "market" "*ri*nok"/**ры́нок**, and represent young, progressively minded professionals, small business owners, and entrepreneurs.

The resurgence of the communist and nationalist parties and the votes that they received in the December 1993 parliamentary elections came as a shocking surprise to many who had expected the reformist parties to win. This resurgence may have been a response to economic difficulties: as inflation skyrocketed, many Russians lost faith in the reformers who were pushing for a free-market economy. National pride was also a factor, as the country lost its international clout and super-power status. The military became dissatisfied; it no longer enjoyed its preeminent position and was forced to absorb units from Eastern Europe and the former republics into already crowded quarters. The rural population from Russia's vast countryside, traditionally conservative, saw no reason to switch and vote for the new reformist groups.

For the December 1999 parliamentary elections the Kremlin created in the fall of 1999 a pro-government party referred to as the Unity Party ("Yedinstvo"/Еди́нство). It became the party to support the candidacy of Vladimir Putin for president; every prime minister before him had a similar power base. This party was formed not for ideological reasons, but to create a progovernment, propresidential bloc in the Duma. By supporting President Putin, the party would benefit.

One of the most important steps taken by this group was the reorganization of the upper house of parliament, the Federation Council. Putin wanted to deprive regional governors of their seats, saying they should attend to their duties in their regions. In the Yeltsin era, these governors ran their regions as personal fiefdoms and often flouted federal laws. In place of the democratically elected governors, the country is divided into seven federal districts, which are controlled by district governors appointed by the president. They are less powerful than the elected regional governors were, and they are responsible to the president. The central government has been strengthened, and the seats in the Federation Council are now filled by members elected by regional (oblast) legislatures.

Russians hope that the new president can improve conditions in Russia, but many are wary of him, assigning to him the term "dark" or "black" horse ("tyomnaya loshadka"/тёмная лоша́дка, "chornaya loshadka"/чёрная лоша́дка). The fact that he was a KGB operative in Dresden in then-Communist East Germany from 1984 to 1990 and in 1998 and 1999 headed this agency (under its new name of Federal Security Service) worries many. "Once you have been a KGB agent you continue to think like a KGB agent," they say. Most people felt that in 2000 there was no viable alternative for president. Almost all political parties support Putin in the early 2000s, some primarily because he is not like his predecessor, Yeltsin, who had squandered the goodwill that the Russian people felt toward him when he emerged as the hero of the new Russia in August

1991. Tired of and disenchanted with Yeltsin toward the end of his presidency, they are hoping that Putin, with his youth, decisiveness, pragmatism, and reputation for being well-organzied and not scarred by corruption, will bring about a better future for the people and that there will be progress and a lessening of smothering bureaucracy and corruption. Above all, Russians hope Putin will bring the war in Chechnya to an end. Some worry about his lack of support for a free media, as evidenced in his battles with the gutsy Vladimir Gusinsky. Gusinsky was jailed at one point for embezzlement (he has since fled abroad), but many believe that his sin, in the government's view, was heading an independent media group (consisting of a television station, NTV; its affiliated radio station, "*E*kho Mos*kvi*"/**Эхо Москвы́**; a magazine, "I*t*ogi"/**Итóги**; and a newspaper, "Sev*o*dnya"/**Сегóдня**) that served as a center of resistance to Putin's politicial machine. In April 2001, NTV was taken over by Gazprom (a state-controlled energy giant), the magazine's entire staff was fired, and the newspaper was shut down. Boris Jordan became the new CEO of NTV. Jordan is an American who grew up in a Sea Cliff, Long Island, community of displaced White Russian aristocrats; he is likened to Joseph Conrad's Colonel Kurtz and dubbed by some the Great Gatsby of Moscow.[2] (See Point 66, "Television and Radio.")

It is important to emphasize that Russia has a presidential form of government with virtually all authority vested in the president, who sits above the three branches of power: Executive (the government headed by the Prime Minister at the pleasure of the president), Legislative (the Duma, which can be disbanded by the president, and the Federation Council, which can be overruled by the Duma), and Judicial (which has no tradition of being fair and independent). With the introduction of the Federal Districts, the presidential control over the provinces got stronger, and there is speculation that the regional governors (oblast level), though popularly elected, could become vulnerable to firing by the president.

---

[2]Brzezinski, Matthew. "American Media Mogul Makes News in Moscow," *The New York Times Magazine,* July 22, 2001.

# 48. PRIVACY

Privacy does not have the importance in a Russian's life that it does for those living in the West. Indeed, the Russian language does not have a word for "privacy." (There is however, an adjective meaning "private.") This is understandable for a society in which the needs and wishes of the "collective" are paramount and in which the word "private" has a negative connotation. Sharing of space and touching are considered positive values, while living an isolated life formerly invited a visit from the authorities. If one has nothing to hide, one does not need privacy. The ruling philosophy is: Live an exposed, explicit life, or you will be exposed.

Students and travelers to Russia who choose the option of staying with host families instead of in dormitories and hotels should be aware that while they will be greeted and treated with great warmth and generosity, areas of the apartments aside from their one private room will be shared with members of the household.

# 49. PUNCTUALITY

The Russian view of punctuality is different from ours. Punching a time clock is an unknown notion for Russians. In a country where for over 70 years job security was ensured and firings were rare, punctuality was of no great importance. A similar attitude exists toward deadlines. The Bolshoi Theater could plan to stage a new production of a ballet on a particular date, but if the director felt that the troupe was not ready, the opening would be put off because artistic considerations would be paramount. In a market-driven economy the show must go on as scheduled, and there would be pressure to meet the scheduled opening date. Similarly, in many a workplace a project might be due the next day, but workers would continue chatting at length about personal matters or leave to do personal shopping. A deadline would not be a high priority for them. Other workplaces, however, do demand punctuality and workers must even work overtime to meet deadlines.

On a social level, if you are invited to dinner at 6:00 PM, do not show up at 6:00 sharp; 6:10, or even 6:20, is quite appropriate.

Theater performances begin and end on time, as do school and university classes. Trains, museums, and shops also adhere strictly to their schedules.

# 50. RELIGION

Outwardly, religion did not seem to play an important role in the Russia of the early 1990s. For over 75 years Russians had been told that religion was the "opium of the people" by its leaders, who proclaimed Russia an atheistic state, following the tenets of Marxism-Leninism. The Russian Orthodox Church, home of Russia's predominant religion before the 1917 Bolshevik Revolution, was severely limited in its ability to spread its message. Those who chose to practice a religion risked discrimination in admittance to institutions of higher learning and at their jobs.

Following the tradition acquired from the Byzantine Empire, when Prince Vladimir chose the Orthodox religion as the state religion in A.D. 998, religion in Russia was closely tied to the state and was subservient to it. This was true in tsarist times as well as during the years of Communist rule. With the advent of glasnost, articles appeared in the Russian press claiming that the Church had been infiltrated by KGB agents.

Prior to the Bolshevik Revolution there were some 5,000 functioning synagogues. Most of these were closed by Stalin, and others were closed by Khrushchev. The practice of Judaism became practically impossible.

In the 1990s, religion in Russia again began playing a more public role. The Russian Orthodox Church slowly became more visible: for the first time in many years Easter and Christmas church services were televised, the press published articles on religious topics, and Bibles in the Russian language and other religious items became available in stores. Religious services took place in churches that the authorities had turned into museums—in Moscow's Kremlin cathedrals and St. Basil's Cathedral. St. Petersburg's Kazan Cathedral, which had become a Museum of the History of Religion and Atheism, was converted into a Museum of the History of West European Christianity and the Orthodox Church. In St. Petersburg the renovation of The Church of the Spilled Blood, which had been "in progress" for about thirty years, was completed, while in Moscow the Cathedral of Christ the Redeemer, blown up on Stalin's orders in 1931, was gloriously rebuilt, a process that started in 1994. The driving force behind the latter was Moscow's mayor, Yury Luzhkov. The plan for 1999 was for Moscow authorities to spend 30 million rubles (about $1,250,000) to renovate 40 religious buildings, among them Russian Orthodox, Catholic, and Lutheran churches and Moslem Mosques.

With the demise of the Soviet Union and the discrediting (for many) of the Communist Party's philosophy, many Russians sought new sources for moral and spiritual guidance. Numerous religions stepped into the vacuum and began proselytizing in Russia; ranging from the Church of the Unification (the "Moonies"), to Hare Krishnas, to Jehovah's Witnesses. Billy Graham made numerous visits to Russia, addressing thousands in stadium settings. The Russian Orthodox Church attempted to stop this flood of missionaries in July 1993, when it lobbied to have Parliament pass a law limiting access of Protestant evangelical groups to Russia. Eventually the restrictions were lifted. Yergin and Gustafson cite a conversation with a Russian Orthodox bishop who claimed that the influx of evangelical missionaries into Russia was a plot by the CIA to destabilize Russia.[3]

At the beginning of the twentieth century, the population shares of religions in the Russian Empire were: Russian Orthodox (71%), Catholic (9%), Muslim (9%), Protestant (5%), and Jewish (3%). According to *The Europa World Yearbook*, in 1997 the principal religious groups in Russia

---

[3]Yergin & Gustafson, *Russia 2010*, p. 64.

were: Russian Orthodox, 75 million; Muslim, 37 million; Roman Catholic, 1,330,000; Buddhist, 1 million; Jewish, 700,000. No figures are given for other Christian sects, such as Baptists, the Armenian Church, and Old Believers. The majority of Muslims are Sunni. (The Russian language distinguishes between ethnic Jewishness and religious Judaism; see Point 53, "Russian Nationality and Citizenship.")

❀

## 51. RESTAURANTS

Since the mid-1990s the restaurant scene in Russia's biggest cities has undergone significant changes. Before 1990, restaurants were far less common in Russia than in the United States. Consequently, it was difficult to get into the restaurants that did exist. In the bigger cities many restaurants were to be found in the Intourist hotels that catered to foreigners. In hotels with several restaurants, the most impressive ones served only those who could pay with foreign currency.

The middle of the 1980s saw the appearance of cooperative restaurants, "kooperativnie restorani"/**кооперативные рестораны**. Families, or a sctrictly regulated number of people, were allowed to renovate an unused space and set up a restaurant. The food in these restaurants was more expensive than in the state-run restaurants. Their main attraction was the attentive service they provided. This type of restaurant no longer exists; it has been replaced by private restaurants with limited-liability partnerships.

When Russians chose to go to a restaurant in large cities, it was frequently to one that offered regional or ethnic cuisine such as the Uzbekistan, Aragvi, and Baku restaurants in Moscow, which served Uzbek, Georgian, and Aizerbaidzhani regional food, though restaurants that specialized in Russian cuisine, such as the Slavic Bazaar, "Slavyanskiy Bazar,"/**Славянский Базар,** were also popular. Outings to the top restaurants were rare for Russians and were reserved for very special occasions. Because it was quite expensive to eat out, they would make an evening of it, ordering extensive appetizers, a main course, and dessert, accompanied by a variety of beverages that might include mineral water, wine, champagne, vodka, and cognac. They expected a slow pace of service, with time, perhaps, for dancing to the restaurant's (generally very loud) orchestra between courses. Many a Russian couple treasures its memories of celebrating a special wedding anniversary or a similarly important occasion at such a restaurant.

But one might ask: What about "middle-class" restaurants, small cafés, fast-food places, and carry-outs, which would delight both a foreign visitor and a native? In the early 1990s, places where one could stop in the evening for a quick bite on the way home from work or on the way to the theater were still rare, though on the increase. By the year 2000, there was a veritable explosion of places to eat, especially in the bigger cities. In addition, fast food of various kinds can be found, either in sit-down places or at street kiosks; hot dogs; "pirozh*ki*"/**пирожки́**, pastries filled with cabbage, potatoes, mushrooms, meat, or sweet cottage cheese; grilled chickens; and wrap sandwiches. Vendors also sell ice cream, even in winter. One can wash down all of this with mineral water, soft drinks, or beer. In Russia's big cities, Japanese sushi bars and Chinese, Indian, Latin American, Italian, and French restaurants are ever more present. In addition, as before, in the theaters ticket holders can purchase open-faced sandwiches of cold cuts, smoked fish, cheese, or caviar to tide them over, with delicious Russian candy ("*Mish*ka"/**Ми́шка**, a favorite individually wrapped chocolate treat) for dessert.

Moscow and other big cities in Russia have their McDonald's restaurants, the number and popularity of which keep increasing. It is not unheard of for a whole class of elementary students to note the end of a school year on McDonald's premises. The Russian fast-food place, Russkoe Bistro, with its signature gold and green colors, is McDonald's worthy competition. The Pizza Huts that attracted many a hungry customer closed their doors during Russia's 1998 monetary crisis.

Those Russians fortunate to have a dining room at their place of work may eat their main meal there. Others eat at a cafeteria-style eating place, called a "Sto*lovaya*," "Die*ti*cheskaya sto*lovaya*," or "Za*ku*sochnaya,"/ **Столо́вая, Диети́ческая столо́вая, Заку́сочная**. They offer a soup, two or three main dishes, and are of acceptable quality, although

Americans might think of them as "greasy spoon" establishments. Some restaurants specialize primarily in one dish, such as "pelmeni"/**пельме́ни**, Siberian meat dumplings.

A visit to Moscow in late 2000 demonstrated the wide variety of restaurants, with varying prices, that await both natives as well as visitors. At "Baravi-M"/**Барави-М**, a French-Russian joint venture near metro station Krasnaya Vorota, a snack for three, which included two teas, a coffee, three mushroom-filled pastries, and three sweet pastries, cost $5.60. Spotlessly clean, with friendly staff, this self-service cafe was perfect for three weary guests who had just met at Moscow's Central Telegraph. At the restaurant chain "*Yolki-Palki*"/**Ёлки-Па́лки**, a main meal for two, at 1:00 PM, with a glass of wine at $2.25 each, cost $36.00, whereas a similar meal, again for two but without wine, at the Metropol Hotel's "European" restaurant cost $67.00. (A glass of tea ranged from 30 cents in the first eatery to $1.00 in the second and $4.00 at the Metropol.) Dinner for three in a Georgian restaurant, "Kav*kazskaya plen*nitsa"/**Кавка́зская пле́нница,** with a bottle of wine for $36.00, came to $127.00. Russian customers, as well as foreign visitors, were enjoying themselves in all of these. Needless to say, however, a pensioner who receives on the average $40.00 a month cannot indulge in any but the first eatery. Many Russians across the land from St. Petersburg to Vladivostok (other than the newly rich and those on generous expense accounts), resent the existence of such eating establishments in which they cannot partake.

For middle and upscale restaurants, reservations are recommended. In Moscow, those desiring help in finding a restaurant can call a restaurant information number, 200-52-31, which suggests various numbers to call for advice. Upon calling 956-66-88, reservations were made at "Kav*kazskaya plen*nitsa" and name and phone number given; a short time later the restaurant called to check on the authenticity of the reservation.

In restaurants everything is à la carte, including bread and butter. In upscale restaurants a service charge may be added; otherwise, one leaves a tip of 15% or so. No tips are expected in inexpensive restaurants, cafes, or bars. Menus will be in Russian, except in the upscale ones, such as Moscow's Savoy, where the menu is in both Russian and English. Prices are given in rubles, unless an artificial conversion unit called "u*slov*naya edi*nit*sa"/**усло́вная едини́ца**, is used. (See Point 70, "Tourist Information.")

In the early 2000s, vegetarianism, "vegetari*an*skaya *pi*shcha"/**вегетариа́нская пи́ща**, is not yet a concept that has taken root in Russia. Even many Russian "salad" dishes such as "Salad Olivier," a Russian potato salad, generally contain meat. However, several dishes, such as beet vinaigrette (pickled beets), or the Georgian dish called "poor man's caviar" ("bakla*zhan*naya ik*ra*"/**баклажа́нная икра́**), a combination of tomatoes, eggplant, and peppers, are ideal for vegetarians. Indeed, Georgian, Indian, Chinese, or Japanese restaurants may be the best choices for vegetarians in Russia. A vegetarian "vegetari*an*ets"/**вегетариа́нец** visitor in Russia may well be advised to bring a supply of athletic energy bars.

Diners who avoid meat but eat eggs, fish, and milk products have additional choices. Russian "pirozhki" come with a variety of fillings, including meat, but also cabbage, potatoes, onions, or mushrooms. Check before eating! Some famous Russian soups, such as "so*lyan*ka"/**соля́нка** and "ras*sol*nik"/**рассо́льник**, are served with fish or meat. Borshch occasionally is prepared vegetarian style. Again, check. "Kule*bya*ka"/**кулебя́ка** is a sort of pie where a mixture of rice, eggs, and mushrooms, plus a main ingredient of either salmon or cabbage, is baked in a pastry. Pancakes, "bli*ni*"/**блины́**, also are ever popular and can be accompanied by sour cream, caviar, smoked salmon, herring, cottage cheese, preserves, sugar, or butter.

Newspapers exist that provide information on restaurant and entertainment possibilities. In Moscow, the Russian-language *Kapital*, on Wednesdays, and the English-language *The Moscow Times* and *The Moscow Tribune*, on Fridays, publish pertinent listings. *The Exile*, an English-language biweekly, is excellent on information about nightlife and eating out. In St. Petersburg, the English-language publications *St. Petersburg Times* and *Where* regularly review and list restaurants.

In these newspapers information can also be gleaned about Moscow's and St. Petersburg's nightclubs and casinos. According to the travel book *The Rough Guide—Moscow*, Moscow has more casinos than any capital in the world.

## 52.   THE RUSSIAN LANGUAGE

Russian is a Slavic language. The Russian alphabet, known as the Cyrillic alphabet, "kir*i*llitsa"/**кири́ллица**, was created in the ninth century by two Slavonic monks, St. Cyril and St. Methodius, based primarily on the Greek and Hebrew alphabets with some letters taken from Glagolitic, an earlier alphabet used to write Old Church Slavonic. The resulting alphabet, after some revision through the ages, consists of 33 letters.[4]

| Cyrillic Letter | | Name | Approximate Pronunciation in English |
| --- | --- | --- | --- |
| А | а | а | car |
| Б | б | бэ | **b**ut |
| В | в | вэ | **v**isa |
| Г | г | гэ | **g**allery |
| Д | д | дэ | **d**octor |
| Е | е | е | **y**et |
| Ё | ё | ё | **y**olk |
| Ж | ж | жэ | mea**s**ure |
| З | з | зэ | vi**s**a |
| И | и | и | v**i**sa |
| Й | й | й (и кра́ткое) ("short" и) | bo**y** |
| К | к | ка | **c**lass, **k**ind |
| Л | л | эл (эль) | **l**uck |
| М | м | эм | **m**other |
| Н | н | эн | co**n**tact, **n**ame |
| О | о | о | **o**ld, n**o**te |
| П | п | пэ | **p**ull |

---

[4]Morris, George W. et al., *Russian Face to Face*, Level 1, Lincolnwood, Illinois: National Textbook Company and Moscow: Russky Yazyk Publishers, 1993, p. 13.

| Cyrillic Letter | | Name | Approximate Pronunciation in English |
|---|---|---|---|
| Р | р | эр | **r**od |
| С | с | эс | **s**it |
| Т | т | тэ | **t**alk |
| У | у | у | f**oo**d |
| Ф | ф | эф | **ph**ilosopher |
| Х | х | ха | **wh**o |
| Ц | ц | цэ | mee**ts** |
| Ч | ч | чэ | **ch**air, mat**ch** |
| Ш | ш | ша | **sh**op |
| Щ | щ | ща | **sh**eep |
| Ъ | ъ | твёрдый знак | hard sign [silent letter] |
| Ы | ы | ы | **ch**arity |
| Ь | ь | мя́гкий знак | soft sign [silent letter] |
| Э | э | э | **e**xcuse |
| Ю | ю | ю | **u**se |
| Я | я | я | **y**ard |

Of these 33 letters, 10 are vowels (five hard—**а, э, ы, о, у**—and five soft—**я, е, и, ё, ю**); 21 are consonants; and 2 are voiceless signs that signal the softness or hardness of the preceding consonant. Five of the consonants have the same sound in both Russian and English (**б, к, м, т, з**), whereas five others are sometimes referred to as "false friends" because although they look exactly like Latin letters, they have a different sound in Russian (**н, р, х, с, в**). An additional six consonants look different from their English equivalents (**д, ф, г, л, п, й**). Finally, there are five consonants that have no English equivalents (**ч, ш, щ, ц, ж**).

Letters can represent one sound or two. The letter **й** placed after a vowel forms a dipthong. Words with more than one syllable have a stress, which may vary in a noun as it is declined (Russian has six cases) or a verb, when conjugated (Russian has six forms for person and number in the present tense). The presence or absence of stress on vowels influences the pronunciation of the vowels. However, Russian is a much more phonetic language than English—by and large it is pronounced the way it is written.

Russian is a language blessed with an extensive vocabulary. Translators and interpreters can attest to this fact; it takes about 10 percent more space and time to translate from English into Russian than from Russian into English.

Russian is spoken by the 150,000,000 people who make up the population of Russia and by the additional 143,000,000 people of the other former republics of the Soviet Union (1992 statistics). Despite the breakup of the Soviet Union, Russian remains the *lingua franca* of the former Soviet republics and of the countries of Eastern Europe. When East Europeans meet, a Hungarian and a Pole are more likely to know Russian than each other's language. Russian is even spoken in areas of Alaska, testimony to the fact that Russia at one time owned this territory.

If you are traveling to Russia, do try to master the Cyrillic alphabet. Signs at airports and train stations, streets, metro stations, and store names will be more comprehensible to you. If you can learn more—vocabulary, useful phrases for various situations, and how the grammar works—so much the better. Friendship and business deals will be easier to achieve. Russians greet attempts at the use of their language with appreciation. So if you are heading for Russia, pick up a Russian textbook, preferably accompanied by a tape, and start practicing.

A word of caution, however, about using Russian in the former republics of the Soviet Union. When addressing a Lithuanian or an Uzbek, for example, it might be wise first to apologize that you do not speak his or her language and then to continue.

The Russian language played a significant role throughout the Soviet Union in eliminating illiteracy, which was at a level of 70 percent in the Russian empire at the time of the Bolshevik Revolution. Through universal education for the entire population, everyone was taught to read and write. In the case of non-Russians, these skills could then be transferred to their native languages.

# 53. RUSSIAN NATIONALITY AND CITIZENSHIP

A Russian internal passport, issued at age 14, identifies a citizen of Russia, giving first and last name, patronymic, and date and place of birth. Prior to 1997, it also indicated nationality or ethnic origin. In Russia, nationality is determined by biological origin. When both parents of a citizen are of the same nationality, i.e., Russian or Georgian, that nationality is indicated on the passport. However, if the parents have different nationalities, such as Russian and Jewish, the person may choose at age 14 which nationality will go into his or her passport. When both parents are Jewish, "Jewish" goes into the passport. Russians consider "Jewish" to be a nationality. The Russian language has two terms: "ev*rey*"/**еврей** to refer to a Jewish male, and "iu*dey*"/**иудей** to indicate a male who is a follower of the Jewish religion. In earlier periods of anti-Semitism, it was easy to identify who was of Jewish origin and to discriminate against them—not to admit them to universities, not to hire them for certain jobs, not to give them promotions. Russians who make a point of indicating a person's Jewishness frequently come across as being anti-Semitic.

Prior to its breakup, over 100 nationalities were comprised in the Soviet Union. Each had its own language, history, religion, culture, national consciousness, and identity. The government strove to foster harmonious relations among the nationalities. By the late 1980s and into the 1990s, frictions—in some cases leading to wars—have come out in the open between a number of the nationalities. The Caucasus region has been especially volatile. A statement made by Dmitry Likhachov, an esteemed Russian academician, illuminates the uneasy relations between the many nationalities of Russia even today: "For me, patriotism is the love of one's country, while nationalism is the hatred of other peoples."[5]

---

[5]Hedrick Smith, *The New Russians*, p. 393.

## 54.  THE RUSSIAN SOUL

In 1866 the poet Fyodor Tyutchev wrote:[6]

| | | |
|---|---|---|
| U*mom* Ros*s*iyu ne pon*yat*, | Russia cannot be understood with the mind, | Умо́м Росси́ю не поня́ть, |
| Ar*sh*inom *ob*shchim ne iz*m*erit; | Or measured with a common yardstick; | Арши́ном о́бщим не изме́рить; |
| U ney *oso*bennaya stat— | She has a unique stature— | У ней осо́бенная стать— |
| V Ros*s*iyu *mozh*no *tol*ko *v*erit. | One must simply believe in Russia. | В Росси́ю мо́жно то́лько ве́рить. |

Whenever a writer cannot explain something about Russians, the writer invariably comments on the mysteriousness of the Russian soul. What is the Russian soul? When did an interest in it appear? To some extent this was the result of the unusual interest in Russia in the middle of the nineteenth century when the works of Russian writers such as Ivan Turgenev (author of *Fathers and Sons*) appeared in Europe. Who or what was Russia? Whatever could not be explained was answered by "Ah, it is the Russian soul!"

When a foreigner immersed in Russian culture thinks of the Russian soul, contradictions come to mind. Illustrative is the character Dmitry Karamazov in Fyodor Dostoevsky's *Brothers Karamazov*. Literary critics sums up his character as generous, depraved, honest, deceitful, and dramatic. The Russian scholar Dmitry Likhachov in his book Za*m*etki o rus*sk*om, *Notes about Russianness* (**Заме́тки о ру́сском**) mentions the Russian love for wide open spaces. He attributes this to the location in Russia of the largest plain in the world. Russians wandered across this vast plain, navigated the big rivers that were part of the plain, and gazed upon the never-ending skies. Russian painters such as Isaak Levitan in his work *Vladimirka* capture this

---

[6]K. Dogdanova, *Ten Russian Poets*, p. 242.

Russian expanse. Russian towns frequently were situated on a high bank of a river, from which the inhabitants could gaze into the distance and into the waters and see the town's reflection and constant motion. When the heavy hand of authority was found to be too oppressive, Russians could choose to lose themselves in the vastness of the plain— going into the forests or setting off for distant Siberia. In such vastness, people become dependent on each other.

Russian generosity and kindness, especially to those in need of aid, are well-known. Foreign visitors, including the American author of this work, are the frequent beneficiaries of this kindness. An inquiry as to where something is located may well result in a Russian personally accompanying the visitor to the desired location. The use of affectionate diminutives is a linguistic expression of Russian kindness.

And while Likhachov acknowledges that many do indeed view Dmitry Karamazov as the embodiment of "Russianness," Likhachov considers early nineteenth-century writer Aleksandr Pushkin as the essence of the Russian soul. Indeed, Dostoevsky himself named Pushkin as the ideal Russian at the 1880 dedication of the Pushkin monument in Moscow.

⚘

## 55. THE SEASONS

In the United States, summer begins with the summer solstice on June 21 or 22, autumn with the autumnal equinox on September 22 or 23, winter with the winter solstice on December 21 or 22, and spring with the vernal equinox about March 21. In Russia the seasons begin on the first of the months indicated above. Hence, summer starts June 1; autumn, September 1; and so forth. The northerly nature of Russia is fully appreciated if one spends August in Moscow. While many cities of the United States are sweltering in the "summer doldrums," Muscovites see the weather turn decidedly fall-like and start to wear fall clothing. In winter, twilight begins around 4:00 in the afternoon.

The northern orientation of Russia's geography contributes to its spectacular "White Nights." During June in St. Petersburg a newspaper can be read without any artificial light as late as midnight, while in Moscow it is still relatively light as late as 10:00 PM.

❁

# 56. SHOPPING

Prior to perestroika the shopping situation for both groceries and merchandise in Russia was predictable, though cumbersome. Instead of supermarkets with their multiple offerings, Russians shopped in separate stores for meat and poultry, milk products, bread, fruits and vegetables, and canned food products. The stores were identified by the store names, such as "Meat," "Bakery," "Fruits and Vegetables." Nonfood items were purchased in department stores. All these stores were owned by the government. Prices were the same in all stores, and there was no bargaining. Foreign visitors could shop "*d*e*lat po*ku*pki"/**делать покупки** in the stores just mentioned, but they could also shop in special stores: Russian government–owned Beriozkas for souvenirs, liquor, and caviar, or for groceries in joint-venture stores, such as Moscow's "Sadko," where only hard currency (U.S. dollars, West German marks, French francs, and so forth) was accepted. Russians could not legally own hard currency and could not shop in these stores.

With the advent of cooperatives in the late 1980s a two-tiered system developed. There were government stores that sold sausage (when it was available) at prices to which the people were accustomed, and there were cooperative stores that sold higher-quality sausage (which was almost always available) at higher prices. Everyone could shop at the "*ri*nki"/**рынки**, or markets, where Russians and people from the former Soviet Union sold produce (vegetables, fruits, honey) from their private plots. In addition, the cooperatives and government stalls sold meat, when available. Bargaining was possible at the markets. To help the population cope with shortages (see Point 57, "Shortages and Deficiencies"), many Russian institutions offered to their employees the privilege of special orders, or "zakazi"/**заказы**. As a result, employees obtained products not generally available to the public.

In the early 1990s, this system completely changed. During the course of a few years all the stores became private, Beriozkas closed, and rubles became the only currency legal for purchases. In 1992 Russia started to convert to a market economy. Shortages ceased to exist; the stores were filled with goods, the majority of them foreign. Supermarkets of the Western variety appeared. The markets mentioned above have expanded to include "veshchevie rinki"/**вещевые рынки**, flea markets, where mostly apparel is sold, as well as "melkooptovie rinki"/**мелкооптовые рынки**, where, in addition to these same items, food and drink items can be obtained at prices lower than those found in stores. Meat products are sold from vans that come directly from meat-processing plants.

From 1992 to 1994 new Russian capitalists emerged who bought merchandise, frequently from abroad, and sold it near metro stations and othe heavy traffic areas. Individuals sold personal items for extra money or purchased items such as shoes, clothing, cigarettes, canned food, bread, or Estée Lauder perfume, added a percentage, and resold the item. Since 1994, some city athorities, dissatisfied with the appearance of this arrangement, have erected stalls, and there are traders with carts from which goods are sold. However, individual selling of items around metro stations still exists.

Foreign visitors, for the most part, prefer to shop in supermarkets, where the quality of goods is higher and there is less risk that goods have been tampered with. Indeed, it is unwise to buy vodka, or any other liquor, without an official seal. For souvenirs of all kinds—fur hats, gzhel ceramics, laser-made objects, and so forth—however, there is no place as much fun as Moscow's Izmailovo Park Market, a glorified flea market. It is open only on weekends. During weekdays, Arbat Street offers the best alternative. In St. Petersburg, the popular shopping areas for tourists are on the famous Nevsky Prospekt. Although vendors are required to accept payment in rubles, dollars on occasion are accepted—depending, that is, on the proximity of the militiaman. If you have a Russian friend who is willing to accompany you for the shopping expedition, follow this procedure: After determining what items you are interested in, step aside and have the native ask—and bargain—for the selling price. It is sure to be lower than if the foreigner had asked for the price: "*Skolko eto stoit?*"/**Ско́лько э́то сто́ит?**

Drugstores, "ap*teki*"/**апте́ки** in Russia sell over-the-counter medications as in the United States. However, cosmetics and other nonmedical products are not sold in Russian *apteki*. Popular antibiotics and allergy, heart, and blood pressure medicine can be obtained in Russian drugstores without a perscription, sometimes at lower prices than in the United States. However, it is important to know the medicine's generic name, because the brand name used in the United States may not be sufficient for identification.

After the financial crisis of August 1998 and the ensuing instability, the availability of foreign food products decreased in Russia for a while, and some restaurants/shops, such as Pizza Hut, left Moscow. In their place appeared products manufactured in Russia by Russian or joint-venture companies. By 2000, however, one could again buy almost anything, especially in the big cities. Stores abound: under Manezh Square in Moscow and on an enclosed "bridge-mall" over the Moskva River as well as in renovated former bomb shelters in Vladivostok. Some items may be unavailable; this foreign visitor could not find Schweppes soda water anywhere in Moscow for a Thanksgiving meal in 2000. Likewise, the unavailability of brown sugar, duct tape, and money pouches (to be worn under one's clothing) has also been noted. However, these are exeptions to the rule. Now goods of all kinds are available: they range from shoddy to the highest quality. For a large part of the population this situation is in direct contrast to the times when they had money in their wallet but there were no desireable goods on the shelves. Those shops that cater to the newly rich Russians, such as Tiffany's, Godiva, Clinique, Dior, Versace, and Benetton, are like salt rubbed in a wound for the ordinary Russian. The status of pensioners is the bleakest. Westerners have long been accustomed to the fact that they cannot afford all the things they see advertised, cannot stay in the fanciest hotels, or go to the most expensive restaurants. To many Russians this is a new reality, and they are resentful.

While shopping in Moscow in the early 2000s, a traveler is struck by the globalization of the world. Disney toys are found everywhere. An American visitor to Moscow searching for three popular Russian toys—Cheburashka, Krokodil Gena, and Kot Leopold—found the former (with great difficulty) but could not find a single Gena the Crocodile or Cat Leopold. Likewise, it was very difficult to find Russian-produced greeting cards, whereas Hallmark cards translated into Russian were everywhere.

As far as payment is concerned, groceries are purchased in supermarkets much as in the Untied States and Europe. At most other stores, however, the buyer chooses the desired items, finds out the cost from a salesperson, then pays a cashier and returns with the receipt to the salesperson to pick up the purchases. Russian cashiers do not put change into the buyer's hand; instead it is placed in a receptacle on the counter. Payment is to be made in rubles. Shops that cater to foreign tourists (and where prices are usually higher) accept credit cards; others do not. Travelers' checks can be changed into rubles only at some banks. (See Point 70, "Tourist Information.")

Many Russian stores, banks, cleaning establishments, drugstores, and service stores close for an hour for lunch, typically between one and three o'clock, but a growing number of grocery stores are open 24 hours a day or at least stay open until 10:00 or 11:00 at night. Lunch breaks do not exist in markets or bazaars; moreover, many of them operate seven days a week. Some stores—even airport stores that cater to tourists and earn greatly desired foreign currency—may be closed for an "inventory: ("*uchot*"/**учёт**) or a "cleaning day" ("sani*tar*niy den"/**санита́рный день**). It behooves the tourist not to leave important purchases until the last day.

## 57. SHORTAGES AND DEFICIENCIES

The end of the 1980s and the early 1990s were years of shortages, or "de-fi*tsit*"/**дефици́т**, when food, clothing, and household items disappeared from the stores. One month it could be soap; another month it could be toilet paper, toothpaste, coffee, tea, underwear, socks, matches, caviar, wine, cooking utensils, toilet seats, paint, or wallpaper. Uncertain of what items would or would not be available, Russian shoppers bought up everything in sight to hoard goods against the day these items became unavailable.

## 58. SLOGANS

Prior to perestroika, slogans and statues everywhere extolled the virtues of the Communist Party. Since 1991 the majority of these slogans and statues have been removed, though Lenin can still be seen, especially in areas of the country where conservative leaders are in power. A similar phenomenon occured with Stalin, who died in 1953. Pictures and statues of Stalin were everywhere. Then in 1956 Khrushchev delivered his "de-Stalinization speech," and in time his portraits and statues disappeared. In 1961 his body was taken out of Moscow's Lenin Mausoleum.

These days Russian cities abound with posters, placards, and banners. Prior to elections, candidates' pictures and their slogans are prevalent. Before holidays such as New Year's, Christmas, and Easter, banners, stretched across streets, wish citizens happy holidays. When Moscow celebrated its 850th anniversary in 1998, banners displayed excerpts from poetry in honor of Moscow; when all of Russia celebrated the 200th anniversary of Aleksandr Pushkin's birth, quotes from Pushkin's works or congratulatory words in his honor were seen throughout Russia.

# 59. SPORTS

The most popular sports in Russia are soccer and hockey. Starting with grade school, Russian youngsters are encouraged to participate in sports. An eighth-grade student in a Moscow school will do some gymnastic exercises in the fall, go cross-country skiing twice a week during the winter season, and in the spring practice "*lyog*kaya at*le*tika," track and field (**лёгкая атлетика**). The gyms of high schools and institutions of higher learning are popular places for students to congregate and for organized groups of youngsters to compete. "Pick-up" squads, randomly gathering, are not a common practice. The American system of after-school intramural sports, or sports competition among schools or universities within a city, is absent in Russia.

Students with an interest in sports attend special sports schools. Prior to the 1990s these schools were supported financially by the Soviet government. Coaches were on the lookout for promising athletes. The ultimate payoff for both the coach and the athlete was a gold medal in the Olympics. In the heyday of Soviet sports, many such medals were earned in gymnastics, track and field, weightlifting, basketball, ice skating, ice dancing, and ice hockey. Sports were used as a measuring stick for the superiority of communism over capitalism. Top athletes received significant perks from the Soviet government—splendid apartments, cars, permission to travel abroad, and cushy jobs. With the breakup of the Soviet Union, many of the athletes from the republics chose to compete under the flags of their own countries. In addition, the government no longer allots the money to sports that it once did.

Traditionally, large factories have encouraged sports among the workers. During nonworking hours, workers can choose to participate in factory-sponsored teams. The most popular sports for workers are soccer and volleyball. Chess, considered a sport, also has its admirers and clubs. If a factory is large, a number of teams may compete with each other, or one factory may compete with another.

Even though the money allotted to train athletes for major competitions has decreased, emphasis on sports remains strong nevertheless.

The maxim "a healthy mind in a healthy body" continues to be popular in Russia.

The disintegration of the former Soviet Union resulted in the disintegration of the teams sent to Olympic competition. The 1992 Olympics saw the Baltic countries competing as separate nations; the majority of the other former Soviet Republics competed for the last time as the "Unified Team." However, if a sportswoman from Ukraine won, the Ukrainian flag, not the Soviet Union flag, was raised. Starting with the 1994 Olympics in Lillehammer, Norway, the former Soviet republics competed under their own flags. At the 2000 Olympics in Sydney, Australia, Russians won 88 medals, 32 of them gold. This was second only to the U.S. team, which won 97 medals, 39 of which were gold.

As before, Russians continue to achieve impressive results at international competitions. Ice dancing, ice skating, gymnastics, and soccer are sports in which Russians excel. Although they compete for their country, some athletes train and even live in Europe or the United States.

For the ordinary Russian the concept of "sports" also encompasses nature activities—not just the very popular cross-country skiing, but also gathering mushrooms (see Point 41, "Mushrooms") and berries.

✿

## 60. STARING

Staring is not considered as impolite in Russia as it is in the United States. Foreign visitors, especially before the 1990s, were stared at in Russia. Since the 1990s, as Western goods have become more available, the distinction between Russians and foreign visitors is less evident. Nevertheless, especially outside the more heavily populated cities of Russia and the former Soviet Union, foreign visitors may still find themselves objects of curiosity. No offense is meant, however. A Russian or a foreign visitor who becomes the object of unwelcome staring can say "Che*vo* vy na me*nya smot*rite?," Why are you staring at me? (**Чего́ вы на меня́ смо́трите?**)

❊

# 61. STREET NAMES AND ADDRESSES

Russian street addresses tend to be much smaller than those in the United States. Buildings are numbered in sequence (even numbers on one side, odd numbers on the other) from the beginning of a street, and this sequence does not depend on "blocks," a concept that is almost non-existent in Russia (see below). As a result, street numbers are lower in Russia than in the United States; it is unusual to have a four- or five-digit building number.

Apartment numbers, on the other hand, are frequently very large. Since some buildings consist of hundreds, sometimes even a thousand apartments, it is possible to have an address such as "Pros*pekt Mi*ra"/ **Проспе́кт Ми́ра**, "dom 317"/**дом** 317, "*kor*pus 4"/**ко́рпус 4**, "kvar*tira* 5227"/**кварти́ра** 5227. If you are given such an address, with "Pros*pekt Mi*ra"/**Проспе́кт Ми́ра** as the street, "dom 317"/**дом** 317 as the equivalent of the idea of a *block*, "*kor*pus 4"/**ко́рпус** 4 as the specific building within the block, "kvar*tira* 5227"/**кварти́ра** 5227 as the apartment number, and you intend to visit, it is wise to ask two questions: what floor, "*etazh*"/**эта́ж**, and what entrance, "pod*ezd*"/**подъе́зд**, you should use. Otherwise, you may spend a long time searching for the right part of the building and the right floor. In addition, many big-city apartment entrances are outfitted with security devices—either "*ko*dovie zam*ki*"/**ко́довые замки́** or "domo*foni*"/**домофо́ны**. In the first case, you punch the code number to unlock the entrance door. In the second case, you punch in a number, and if the person whom you are visiting is at home, he or she will respond to your summons and electronically allow you to open the door.

When a house is located at the crossing of two streets, the address indicates this fact. Thus, "*Plot*nikov pere*ulok*, Dom 2/8"/**Пло́тников** переу́лок, Дом 2/8, means that the house is number 2 on the Plotnikov Street, but number 8 on the street that it crosses. The name of this secondary street is not given in an address.

(See Point 37, "Letters, Greeting Cards, and Announcements," on how to address correspondence to Russians.)

✿

# 62. THE "STRONG MAN" CONCEPT

The concept of the "strong man"—"*sil*naya *lich*nost," "*sil*naya ru*ka*," "*tvyor*daya ru*ka*" (си́льная ли́чность, си́льная рука́, твёрдая рука́)—is well known in Russian culture. The attitude toward Ivan the Terrible, Stalin, and other leaders in Russian history is tied to the Russian attitude toward the strong man, whoever he may be. The idea started with fairy tales and how they presented the image of the tsar. Peasants, often abused by overbearing, inconsiderate landlords, believed that landlords could abuse them only because the tsar did not know about their actions. "If only he knew about it, he would do something." After the Bolshevik Revolution, during the period of Stalin's excesses, his victims went to their deaths believing that Stalin's enemies, not Stalin, were responsible for their unjust treatment. The West values individualism and freedom and mistrusts authority. Russians value order and security and believe that firmness from their leaders is essential.

✿

# 63. SUPERSTITIONS

A variety of superstitions influence the behavior of Russians. Prior to leaving for a trip, they sit down in silence for a few minutes. Failure to do so, it is believed, will result in some calamity, conveyed by the expression "ne *bu*det do*r*ogi"/**не бу́дет доро́ги** (literally "you will have no road"). Once one leaves the house, it is considered bad luck to return for any reason. Should one be forced to return, however, danger can be averted by looking in the mirror before one leaves the house the second time.

It is important for Russians not to appear to be joyous about something ahead of time, lest the evil eye fall on them. They knock on wood three times, or spit over the left shoulder, or say "*shto*bi ne *sglazi*t," so that no one will curse them (**чтобы не сгла́зить**). Birthday wishes or wedding anniversary congratulations are not conveyed ahead of the actual day of celebration. Expectant mothers do not purchase anything for their babies until they are born, lest the evil eye harm the baby. After a baby is born, some parents choose not to show the baby to anyone for two or three weeks so that no one can harm it by complimenting it.

Russians do not sit at the corner of a table or shake hands over a threshold. Salt spilled on the table means there will be a fight in the family. A broken mirror portends some kind of misfortune. If a bird flies into a room, there will be a death in one's closest circle. If a cat, especially a black one, crosses the street, Russians believe that to avoid misfortune they should change the direction in which they are going, or wait until someone else walks in front of them. A spider crawling up a wall forecasts good news; one crawling down, bad news. A Russian whose left palm itches expects to receive some money. If the left nostril itches, however, some imbibing will soon take place. If a knife falls, a male visitor can be expected; if it is either a spoon or a fork, a female visitor.

If two friends accidentally knock heads, they should immediately knock heads again, otherwise there will be an argument between them. Likewise, if a person steps on someone's foot, that person should step on the foot of the person who origianlly misstepped, or an argument will take place between them. Russians who give medicine or a sharp object as a gift to someone are given some token money for the item because it is "permitted" to "sell" such items but not to give them as gifts.

# 64. TEA

Tea, "chay"/**чай**, has been the most popular nonalcoholic drink in Russia, consumed by both adults and children, ever since it arrived from Mongolia in the seventeenth century. Tea is taken with breakfast, after the midday meal (dinner for Russians—see point 38, "Meals and Mealtimes"), at midafternoon break, and after supper. (Tea with a meal is highly unusual; no amount of pleading at Intourist restaurants, for example, would produce tea until dessert was served.) Except for the Krasnodar region, Russia does not produce its own tea. Prior to the breakup of the Soviet Union, tea from the Georgian Republic was sold; its green tea was considered medicinal. The most popular tea is imported from India and Sri Lanka. Of English and American teas, Earl Grey is a special favorite of Russians. These days any good tea is an appreciated gift.

Although the preparation of tea is not as important in Russia as it is in Japan, certain traditions are nevertheless preserved. Loose tea is placed in a scalded teapot, hot water is poured over it, and a tea cozy, sometimes called a "*grel*ka"/**грéлка** ("heater") but more typically "*b*aba na *chay*nik/ **бáба на чáйник** (old woman on the teapot), is placed over the teapot. After the tea has been steeped for a few minutes, a little of the strong mixture is poured into teacups or into a glass in a metal holder called a "podsta*kan*nik"/**подстакáнник**, and boiling water is added to taste. Individual tea bags are now available, but Russians do not consider such tea real tea!

The traditional way of serving tea is through the use of a samovar, "samo*var*"/**самовáр**, literally "self-boiler," an urnlike metal container in which water is heated. Electric samovars appeared in the twentieth century. The traditional ones, however, contain a cylindrical tube into which hot coals are placed to heat the water. A strong tea mixture, "za*var*ka"/**завáрка**, is prepared in a small teapot. Tea is served by pouring a bit of the "za*var*ka" into a glass, then adding water from the samovar. When not in use, the teapot is placed on top of the samovar, and a tea cozy is placed on top of it.

# 65. TELEPHONE (AND MAIL)

## Telephone

The first telephone was installed in Russia in 1896. In spite of progress made in the installation of new and the renovation of old technology, communication facilities are not consistently high quality in Russia, especially outside its main cities. A frequently heard expression is "Vy ne tu*da* po*p*ali," "You didn't land where you expected"; that is, you reached the wrong party (**Вы не туда́ попа́ли**). After one reaches the desired party, the phone conversation may still be unsatisfactory because of static on the line. Phone conversations are frequently cut off. Hence the unnerving tendency of Russians to say "allo, allo"/**алло́, алло́**, to verify that a connection still exists, at the slightest pause in a conversation. Nevertheless, those who have telephones are grateful. (According to official Soviet data, in 1986 only 28 percent of urban and 9.2 percent of rural families had telephones). Not infrequently, in business, dormitories, and communal housing there exist communal telephones that are shared over a number of floors. In such cases one needs to call several times until the right party picks up the telephone.

For people living in Russian villages or spending a few days at their dachas, communication with the outside is possible from post offices, which have one or two phone booths with long-distance connections. A person who wants to make a phone call fills out a form indicating the place to be called, the desired phone number, and the number of minutes the conversation is expected to take. The person pays in advance for the conversation and waits until called to go to the booth. If the party called is not available, of if the phone conversation takes less time than expected, a refund is in order. Within cities, phone calls are made at pay phones which require a pay phone calling card or a token. The cards come in various ruble units, from 25 to 1000, and can be purchased at metro stations, kiosks, and post offices. A sixty-minute card in 2000 cost 104 rubles, or $3.80. These places also sell tokens, "zhe*to*ni"/**жето́ны**, which are still used in some pay phones, especially in smaller cities.

Phone conversations tend to be brief in Russia, except when talking about mundane matters. The frequently poor quality of phone connections plays a role. So does the desire to exchange information face to face, not via telephone. Fear that the telephone may still be bugged—and the certainty that it has been bugged in the past—keep Russians from revealing anything of importance on the telephone.

Travelers who arrive in Russia without the home phone numbers of those they want to call may find it difficult to obtain them. Public telephones do not have telephone directories. The existence of residential telephone directories is sporadic. Smaller towns are more likely to have them than big cities; however, to keep those directories updated yearly, supplements need to be purchased. In the big cities, if one has access to computers, one can purchase pirated (from Russian police records) CD-ROM telephone directories. Otherwise, to get a phone number, you need to go to a "*Spra*vochnoe byu*ro*," Information Bureau (**Спра́вочное бюро́**), give the person's name and year of birth, pay a small fee, and return a few hours later for the information. It is said that offices and libraries in Moscow have directories with residential phone numbers, but recent visitors to Moscow report that neither the Moscow State University nor the Lenin Library had such a directory.

"Yellow Pages" telephone books have been available in limited editions in the largest cities since the 1960s. In the 1970s the telephone company in Moscow instituted an "Information" number, 09, by which operators gave out desired governmental phone numbers. In the late 1990s, the number 05 could be called for information on Moscow's private firms at a charge of 17 rubles. The 1990s saw numerous business phone books published by foreign companies.

Russians answer the telephone with one of these three statements: "Da?"/"Al*lo*"/"*Slu*shayu vas," Yes?/Hello/I am listening to you (**Да?/Алло́/ Слу́шаю вас**). Conversations, as mentioned above, tend to be brief. When calling a store to find out its hours, for example, it behooves one to listen carefully, because having given an answer, the person will immediately hang up, not giving the caller a chance to verify the information.

When Russians give a telephone number, they say the first three digits as a unit, followed by the next two as a unit, and again the last two as a unit. Thus 435-34-98 would be "four hundred thirty five/thirty-four/ninety-eight."

For a traveler to Russia. the following information may be of special interest. The number of answering machines, "avtoot*vet*chiki" (**автоотве́тчики**), is increasing rapidly, as is that of pagers, "*pey*dzheri" (**пе́йджеры**). Likewise, foreign-made portable phones, "mo*bil*nie tele*foni*" (**моби́льные телефо́ны**), both cellular ("*so*tovie"/**со́товые**) and—much rarer, because they are so much more expensive—satellite ("*sput*nikovie"/**спу́тниковые**), are growing in popularity, which alleviates communication problems. In the late 1990s, a typical monthly charge for a pager was $12 to $20, while for a cell phone the base monthly charge was $20 to $30, plus 30 cents per minute. It is easy to send and receive faxes, not only from Moscow and St. Petersburg but even from cities such as Kazan. Hotels have fax capability, as do many railway stations. A two-page fax from Moscow's Central Telegraph to Baltimore cost 110 rubles, or about $3.90, at the end of 2000. One can also receive faxes at the Central Telegraph in Moscow. From the United States it is necessary to dial 007-095-925-86-07. In 2000, the charge to receive a fax was 5 rubles or 17 cents.

Internet salons are plentiful in Russia's cities. An hour's use in Moscow's Lenin Library cost about a dollar in the late 1990s; in St. Petersburg's Intercity International Telephone Center, about $5.00; and about $4.00 from a Vladivostok hotel in the early 2000s. Dial-up Internet service is also widely available, with many service providers, such as Glasnet, competing for customers. The costs are about $6 to $10 per month.

It is possible, and not very difficult, to direct-dial Europe, the United States, and similar locations from certain areas of Russia, such as Moscow, St. Petersburg, and Novosibirsk. While in Russia, to call the United States from a private phone one dials 8, waits for a dial tone, then 10 for an international line, 1 for the United States, followed by area code and phone number. One may also contact operators from the United States by dialing an access number and giving the American operator a credit card number. AT&T can be reached in Moscow at 755-50-42 and in St. Petersburg at 325-50-42. MCI and Sprint also have access numbers. Such calls are fast, efficient—and expensive. To call an

800 number from Russia, a calling card is needed, and an international phone fee will be charged. Travelers calling from Russian hotels should make certain ahead of time as to what the charges will be, because prices vary greatly.

## Mail

Although there has been improvement, especially in Moscow, in the quality of its phone service, the same cannot be said about Russia's postal system when it comes to international mail, which is slow and unreliable to and from Russia. In mid-2001, under "Mail," the Travel Guide on *The Moscow Times*' web site (http://www.moscowtimes.ru) stated: "Russia has plenty of mailboxes and post offices, but they're only useful for letters that don't need to arrive within a month and wouldn't be missed if they never arrived." However, it is easy to send express mail to and from major cities, as courier companies such as Federal Express and DHL Worldwide Service have offices in Russia. A 7-ounce mailing from Moscow to the United States cost $48 via DHL in the late 1990s and took about four days. Occasionally customs can hold up a package a bit longer.

❦

# 66. TELEVISION AND RADIO

The Russian word for a television set is "tele*vizor*"/**телеви́зор**, and the word for television broadcasting industry is "tele*videnie*"/**телеви́дение**. Russians love to watch television, "smo*tret* televizor"/**смотре́ть телеви́зор**. If they want to know what is on television, they ask "What is going (lit.) on television?" "Shto i*dyot* po televizoru?"/**что идёт по телеви́зору?**

Russia has three dominant national television stations/channels. Of the three, two are owned by the government: ORT, "Ob*shchest*vennoe Ros*si*yskoe Tele*videnie*"/**Обще́ственное Росси́йское Телеви́дение**

(Channel 1), and RTR, "Ros*si*yskoe Tele*vi*denie i *R*adio"/**Росси́йское Телеви́дение и Ра́дио** (Channel 2). ORT has not changed its offical Soviet style of presenting the news, and many of the shows are holdovers from the Brezhnev era. The third channel, NTV, "Neza*vi*simoe Tele*vi*denie"/**Незави́симое Телеви́дение** (Channel 4), belonged until April 2001 to the company "Media-MOST"; it was independent of government control, and indeed it and its leader Vladimir Gusinsky frequently were at significant loggerheads with the government, especially regarding NTV's coverage of the war in Chechnya. (See Point 47, "Politics and Parties.") NTV was created from scratch, with participation of American capital and know-how and the latest technology. It was the most professional TV channel in Russia, coming very close to Western standards for fair and objective news reporting.

The schedule of stations consists of news, films, music, talk shows, sports events, sitcoms, and game shows. In the morning, news is shown every five to ten minutes between programs similar to "Today" and "Good Morning, America," as well as stories of general interest, interviews, and cartoons. During the day, old films are shown, as well as reruns of sitcoms, programs shown the previous evening, and short news segments. During the evening prime time (from 7:00 to 10:00) the main new programs are shown, as well as analytical political programs and entertainment features.

Programs dealing with politics are popular in Russia. Before the change at NTV, the best known anchors and programs were Nikolai Svanidze on RTP's "Window" ("*Z*er*k*alo"/**Зе́ркало**); Evgeny Kiselyov on NTV's "Roundup" ("I*t*ogi"/**Ито́ги**); and Svetlana Sorokina on NTV's "Hero of the Day" ("Ge*roy* dnya"/**Геро́й дня**), which featured one-on-one interviews with political and cultural figures. Two NTV programs that satirized politicians were especially popular: "Ito*go*"/**Итого́** ("Altogether") and "*K*u*k*li"/**Ку́клы** ("Puppets"). On the latter show, puppets in the likeness of various politicians appeared in satirical skits; on the former, anchor Viktor Shenderovich, in the manner of "Saturday Night Live," satirized actions and statements made by politicians in the course of the current week. The government had made several attempts to take the show "Kukli" to court for its sharp criticism of it. Since the April 2001 takeover of NTV the situation with these anchors and programs is in a state of flux. Kiselyov moved to Channel 6, a local Moscow station. (Immediately the government found reason to question the station's financial affairs.) Other anchors have also switched channels, sometimes more than once. In late 2001 it is difficult to predict the orientation that programs such as "Kukli" will take.

Many Russian television programs are imitative of American and European programs. For example, "*Pole* chu*des*"/**Поле чудес** resembles *Wheel of Fortune*, and "*Svoya igra*"/**Своя игра** corresponds to *Jeopardy!* In the early 2000s, "O, schast*livch*ik!"/**O, счастливчик!**, modeled on *Who Wants to Be a Millionaire*, enjoyed great popularity. In 2001 this show, now renamed in Russian the more familiar "Who Wants to Be a Millionaire," "Kto *kho*chet bit milli*o*nerom"/**Кто хочет быть миллионером**, moved from NTV to ORT. This move was not because of politics, but the result of ORT outbidding NTV for the British license for 2001.

"Travelers' Club" ("Klub pute*shest*vennikov"/**Клуб путешественников**), has enjoyed popularity for over thirty years, as has "Good Night, Little Ones!" ("Spo*koy*noy *no*chi, mali*shi*!"/**Спокойной ночи, малыши!**). The cartoon characters of the latter show—the piglet Khryusha, the dog Filya, and the rabbit Stepashka—are as popular with Russian children as the characters on *Sesame Street* are with American children. (The latter program appears in locally produced versions as "*U*litsa Sez*am*"/**Улица Сезам**.) Other programs that have demonstrated their popularity for over 25 years are "What? Where? When?" ("Shto? Gde? Kog*da*?"/**Что? Где? Когда?**), a variation of *College Bowl*, and "KVN"/**КВН**, "Klub ve*syo*likh i na*khod*chivikh"/**Клуб весёлых и находчивых**, literally "Club of Lively and Quick-Witted (People)," in which groups of young people compete with each other in composing and performing musical and humoristic presentations. Most foreigners are struck by the fact that Russians of all classes love serial soap operas, "*mil*nie *op*eri"/**мыльные оперы**. They are imported from Mexico, Brazil, and the United States and are dubbed into Russian. They are shown in prime time in the evenings and repeated the next day on daytime TV. In the late 1980s and the beginning of the 1990s a largely unsuccessful attempt was made to produce Russian soap operas. More successful have been Russian-produced detective series: "Streets of Broken Lamplights" ("*U*litsi raz*bi*tikh fona*rey*"/

**Улицы разбитых фонарей**), "Lethal Power" ("U*boy*naya sila"/**Убойная сила**), and "Criminal Petersburg" ("Ban*dit*skiy Peters*burg*"/**Бандитский Петербург**).

The most popular sports programs show soccer and ice hockey games. Less popular are recent additions to the sports scene: Formula 1 car races, volleyball, basketball, and tennis.

Besides the three dominant channels, many additional channels exist. Most regions of Russia also have a local channel, which concentrates on local features, and various other channels.

As of the early 2000s, there are also about ten satellite television stations. Their cost—about $350 for a dish, and subscription fees of $30/$40 per month—means only the richer Russians can afford to watch these stations and their special sports, children's cartoon, and CNN programs.

In recent news programs, Russian TV has become as "sensation" oriented as the West and can be very graphic. Broadcasts start out with news about the latest fires and other calamities. Moscow's TV station (Channel 3) has an 11:45 PM program, "P*etrov*ka Street, 38"/**Петровка, 38** (the address of the Moscow headquarters of the Criminal Investigation Department) which details the criminal activities of the day. Channel 4 had a 6:40 PM newscast, "Gor*ya*chaya *khro*nika s *mes*ta prois*shest*viya"/**Горячая хроника с места происшествия**, "Live from the Scene of Action."

TV listings can be found in most newspapers and in publications similar to the *TV Guide* in the United States. In addition, the English-language newspaper *The Moscow Times* publishes TV listings in its Saturday edition.

Hotels in Russia offer Western channels, including CNN, BBC, Europort, and NBC, as well as a wide range of Russian ones.

When referring to "radio" as a broadcasting medium, the Russian word for it is "*radio*"/**радио**, a term that is also used for the apparatus. However, if one wants to specify "radio" as a receiving set, it will be referred to as "radiopri*yom*nik"/**радиоприёмник**.

Russians, not unlike Americans, like to listen to radio, "*slu*shat *radio*"/**слушать радио**—most of all "*mezh*du *delom*"/**между делом**, while doing other things: working at one's job, driving to or from work, preparing meals. In some offices the radio is on the entire day. Music, news, advertisements, and call-ins predominate. People choose to listen to one station or another based on the station's musical orientation. Some radio stations have preserved a pre-perestroika form; on these programs, similar to National Public Radio programs in the United States, one can hear analytical commentary on cultural and political events, discussions, and the readings of literary works. Many consider The Echo of Moscow "Ekho Moskvi"/Эхо Москвы to be the best radio station in Moscow. It is unknown how the takeover of Gusinsky's independent media group will affect it. The best way to receive news in English on the radio is to listen to shortwave BBC and Voice of America broadcasts.

Television is by far the most important mass medium in Russia. Many Russians and foreign observers were judging President Putin's commitment to democracy by how much freedom he allowed independent NTV, the only television station to deliver news in an objective and unbiased manner. With NTV's takeover in April 2001 by Gazprom, the state-controlled energy giant, national television in Russia again, for the time being, became a tool of official propoganda.

## 67. TEMPERATURE

Temperature in Russia is measured in degrees of Celsius (centigrade). To convert to the Fahrenheit scale, multiply the Celsius temperature by 9/5, and then add 32.

Russia is a vast country with eleven time zones. The entire country is farther north than Los Angeles. Both St. Petersburg and Moscow lie to the north of Quebec, Canada. Average high (Fahrenheit) temperatures in three Russian cities are:

|          | Moscow | St. Petersburg | Irkutsk (Siberia) |
|----------|--------|----------------|-------------------|
| January  | 14     | 23             | 9                 |
| February | 19     | 24             | 7                 |
| March    | 29     | 33             | 21                |

|  | Moscow | St. Petersburg | Irkutsk (Siberia) |
|---|---|---|---|
| April | 43 | 45 | 36 |
| May | 60 | 58 | 52 |
| June | 67 | 66 | 67 |
| July | 71 | 71 | 70 |
| August | 68 | 66 | 66 |
| September | 56 | 57 | 52 |
| October | 44 | 45 | 38 |
| November | 28 | 34 | 4 |
| December | 17 | 26 | 3 |

The northern orientation of Moscow should not be taken as an indication that long underwear is in order when planning a visit. Russians like to have their apartments, houses, places of work, metro stations, and other buildings, considerably warmer than Americans do. Inside buildings long underwear may make one uncomfortably warm. From October to early April what is essential is that one have a warm long coat, hat, scarf, gloves, and high, sturdy, waterproof boots.

⚘

## 68. TIME OF DAY

In Russia the 24-hour system is used to give the official time for travel timetables, as well as for television schedules, theater performances, film showings, and sports events.

The 24-hour system is also frequently used in everyday conversations. A 4:00 PM social get-together or a business appointment is at "16 hours" for a Russian. (If the time mentioned is after 12 noon, just subtract 12 from the quoted time to determine the hour.)

When the 24-hour system is not used, Russian, which does not use AM and PM, follows the clock time with the genitive case of *morning, day, evening,* and *night:* "ut*ra*"(**утра́**), "dnya" (**дня**), "*vechera*" (**ве́чера**), and "*no*chi" (**но́чи**). Although the Russian system of telling time is rather complicated, with different grammar rules for time up to the half hour and after it, the popularity of digital watches and clocks has made it acceptable to say "che*ti*re *so*rok pyat," 45 minutes after 4 (**четы́ре со́рок пять**), as opposed to "bez *che*tverti pyat," a quarter to five (**без че́тверти пять**), literally "five without a quarter."

In a written time, a period is placed between the hour and the minutes, instead of a colon: 4.16.

## 69. TOILETS

Foreign visitors should be aware that the condition of Russian public toilets can frequently be a source of consternation. In out-of the-way places, even those frequently visited by tourists, toilets may be no more than a hole in the ground in a wooden shack. Even where modern plumbing exists, the toilets are frequently dirty and there is no toilet paper. One should always carry one's own tissue. In several theater visits in late 2000 a visitor found no toilet paper available in theater toilet stalls even *before* the performances. Pay toilets, however, are the exception to the rule—where available, they are carefully maintained with toilet paper (one may need to ask for it from an attendant), soap, and so forth. Russians consider it worth the rubles charged to use these clean facilities. Preferable are the no-charge clean restrooms in Western restaurants such as McDonald's. Foreign visitors should follow suit.

# 70. TOURIST INFORMATION

## Visas

A visa, "*viza*"/**виза**, is required for all foreigners (except citizens of some of the former Soviet republics) entering Russia. If one is part of a package tour group, the tour agency will obtain the visas for its clients. However, those traveling as individuals need proof of prebooked accommodations (at least for one night) or an invitation from a tour company, a business/educational institution, or an individual. Visas can be obtained through the Russian Embassy, which can be a time-consuming and complex process, or through a travel agency, which will do the legwork for a fee. The specific dates of entering and leaving Russia and the planned itinerary must be provided. The specific dates will appear on the visa, but, in contrast to previous years, in the 2000s the individual Russian cities are not listed. It normally takes ten working days to obtain a visa, but an extra fee will produce it in two days or so.

According to government regulations, travelers staying for more than three days in Russia need to register their visas with OVIR (Visa Registration department). Hotels frequently handle this for their guests. Many independent travelers do not comply; however, if there are any irregularities with a visit, this lack of registration can cause a fine and delays in leaving Russia.

To extend a visa, a statement requesting the extension is required from the person or organization that issued the initial invitation. Hence it is especially important to know who or what organization extended the visa invitation. Without written permission for an extension, travelers arriving at an airport may be denied boarding and sent back for the necessary paperwork. A fine may also be imposed.

Those planning to stay in Russia for more than three months need to present a certificate proving that they are not HIV-positive. The certificate, written in both English and Russian, must contain the applicant's passport information, proposed length of stay in Russia, and blood test results for HIV infection, including date of the test, signature of the doctor conducting the test, medical examination results, diagnostic series, and seal of the hospital/medical organization.

Upon receiving a visa, with its entrance, "vezd"/**въезд**, and exit, "*viezd*"/**въіезд**, parts, it is wise to photocopy it. The visa should be placed in one's passport and kept there while one is in Russia. The photocopy should be kept separately.

## Customs, "Ta*mozh*nya"/тамо́жня

Upon entering Russia, one must pass a customs inspection, "prokho*dit* ta*mozh*enniy os*motr*"/**проходи́ть тамо́женный осмо́тр**. The first task is to fill out a customs declaration form, frequently handed out on plane or train and, hopefully, in English! Beyond personal information such as name and address, the form asks information on how much and what kind of money the traveler is bringing in, including travelers' checks. Jewelry of precious metals and stones is to be listed. If one is taking technology, such as computers, or musical instruments, it is wise to list them.

The next step is to present the passport, together with the customs declaration, to a customs inspector, "ta*mozh*enniy nads*mot*rshchik"/**тамо́женный надсмо́трщик**. Travelers may be asked to show money and other items they are declaring. The inspector may ask that luggage be opened, or the luggage may be passed on a conveyor belt through an x-ray machine or just waved through. It is not wise to bring in unusually large amounts of the same item—officials may take that as a sign that the item will be sold in Russia and may levy a duty, "*posh*lina"/**по́шлина**, on the items. Documentation for prescription drugs is a wise thing to have, especially if there are many. It is a felony to bring narcotics into Russia, and the U.S. govenrment will not aid a U.S. citizen so accused.

Upon leaving Russia, travelers fill out another customs declaration, accounting for money currently in their possession and providing a listing of the jewelry as mentioned above. This declaration is presented together with the one that was filled out upon entering Russia. Customs officials may ask that money that is being taken out be shown. It is illegal to take out more money than one has brought in, and it is imperative that the same jewelry, technology, etc., that was brought in leaves the country. If, as the American author of this book once did, a traveler brings, by arrangement, a computer from an American educational institution to give to a Russian institution, make certain to obtain documentation from both parties.

When a traveler leaves Russia, the customs inspectors may search luggage by hand, examine it with an x-ray machine, or just let it pass. It is wise to have documentation at hand for large purchases, in case one is questioned. The Russian government is on guard against tourists taking out valuable works of art and, especially, on the lookout for speculators, who may be selling them in the West. Travelers purchasing old books (printed before 1945), paintings, drawings, sculpture, furniture, fabric, manuscripts, antique coins and currency, or objects of archaeological value for export need to obtain official permission, which includes paying a 100 percent tax of government-assessed value. Old icons and samovars (as opposed to modern reproductions) may not leave the country at all, unless they have been purchased with export certificates. Items containing precious metals and stones are likewise under special protection. It is always wise to check the latest Russian laws regarding customs regulations.

## Luggage, "ba*gazh*"/багáж

Two suitcases, "chemo*dani*"/чемодáны (total dimensions, height + depth + width, not to exceed 106 inches and no dimension to exceed 62 inches), weighing up to 70 pounds each, can be checked by international air travelers, with a carry-on of no more than 18 pounds (46 inches total). If a traveler exceeds these limitations or has additional luggage, the fees can be as high as $100 per item. Officially, these regulations apply to coach/economy class as well as business and first class. Experience has proven, however, that the airlines are frequently more generous with travelers in the last two categories, allowing additional luggage to be checked for free. Within Russia and Eastern Europe, however, some of the airlines allow considerably less poundage before charging for additional weight, so it behooves one to check on the policies of individual airlines. Travelers are advised to bring extra luggage identification tags, especially for luggage sporting the red/white/blue American Tourister tags, which tend to disappear. (Or perhaps it is best not to use those tags at all in Russia.) Luggage should be durable and have a sturdy lock, "za*mok*"/**замо́к**, to be used while the luggage is checked as well as when it is in a hotel or other place of residence.

Unless one relies on a hotel's safe, a traveler's passport, visa, airline ticket, and money should be carried at all times in a money belt or pouch worn under clothing. Buy these articles prior to arriving in Russia; they may be difficult to find there. Avoid a fanny pack.

## Accommodations

Most travelers to Russia stay in a hotel, "gos*t*initsa"/**гости́ница**. The hotel situation in Russia in the 2000s is significantly different from that in the previous decades, especially in its principal cities and in the higher-bracket/luxury hotels. Whereas, prior to 1990, generally the only choice was government Intourist-run hotels, which offered acceptable accommodations but few frills, in the early 2000s a variety of hotels, generally built under joint Russian-Western ventures, have enriched the hotel scene. The new hotels offer services such as a choice of restaurants and bars, fitness centers with saunas and swimming pools, and business centers. Some of the latter are open 24 hours a day and offer Internet, fax, computer rental, printing, scanning, interpreting, translation, and secretarial services. Arrangements can be made for car rental.

Even with the extensive construction that has taken place in the big cities, there is nevertheless a shortage of hotels, especially in the modest price range. Along with the increased luxury and services offered by the newly constructed or renovated hotels has come a significant increase in prices. A double room, "*nomer*/*kom*nata na dvo*ikh*"/**но́мер/ко́мната на двои́х**, in a luxury Moscow or St. Petersburg hotel, such as the Metropol in Moscow and the Evropeiskaya in St. Petersburg, costs $240 plus VAT, which can be as much as 20 percent or more. The cost for a deluxe room in Moscow's Renaissance hotel ranges from $300 to $600. The hotels that cater to well-heeled foreign guests sometimes include breakfast in the cost of the room; more modest hotels generally do not. A traveler should check upon making reservations. Dinners in the spectacular dining rooms of the grand hotels can be quite expensive. (See Point 51, "Restaurants.")

Of the older Soviet-era hotels, such as Moscow's Kosmos, Leningradskaya, Minsk, and Rossiya, most charge one price for Russians and a different, higher price for foreigners. In some cases this also applies to meals. (A recent traveler to Hawaii noted that a two-tiered pricing also occurs in Hawaii; airline tickets on Hawaiian and Aloha Airlines are considerably discounted for permanent residents.)

The luxury hotels accept all the major credit cards, but it is wise to take along two, just to be safe. Many of the more modest hotels do not take credit cards. Almost none accept travelers' checks, although a nearby bank may cash them.

It is possible to order a room via telephone or fax. However, going through a travel agent may result in lower rates. Business travelers should check whether their company can negotiate lower rates, especially with luxury hotels. Many of the hotels have web sites and can be reached via Internet.

Adventurous travelers who are in Russia for an extended period of time, such as graduate students, when they arrive in a city by train, have reported finding space in an inexpensive hotel or a private room by finding a "babushka" with a sign around her neck that says "accommodations" and negotiating with her. The prices they quoted were very reasonable, around $10. This is for the brave—and those who speak Russian.

## Disabled Travelers

Disabled travelers will have a difficult time coping in Russia. Public transportation makes no allowances for those unable to navigate buses and metros. Entrances to museums, theaters, and sports events may likewise be problematic. The vast majority of hotels cannot accommodate disabled travelers. Some of the Moscow luxury hotels (Savoy, Metropol), however, when queried, stated that they have special rooms for the disabled.

While riding the metro, a traveler may see on occasion a disabled person in a wheelchair wheeled by a helper through the metro's cars, asking for alms. However, this does not mean that access exists for disabled persons to the metro. The disabled persons, as well as their wheelchairs, are hand-carried down the escalator by persons assigned to this job, and then the handicapped are wheeled from one car to another. The money they garner goes to an organization that offers them room and board, in exchange for the money they gather.

## Electricity

Electrical power in Russia is supplied at 220 volts. In order to use an American appliance, that accepts 110-volt power, a 220–110 V current adaptor, "*adap*ter"/**адáптер**, is needed, as well as a two-plug converter, "kon*ver*ter" **конвéртер**, to plug in the appliance. Some travelers have reported difficulty with the thickness of the plugs, because most European plugs are thicker than those used in Russia. Travelers staying in the more modern Russian hotels should not experience this problem.

## Mosquitoes

Many travelers have been made miserable by these pesky insects (ko-ma*ri*/**комары́**), especially from June to early October. Even major hotels, such as the Rossiya in Moscow, can be plagued by mosquitoes on lower floors on spring and summer evenings, because windows are unscreened. Although the American author of this book has been to Russia some thirty times, she has fortunately never been subjugated to the mosquito's bite there, whereas the "no-see-ums" and mosquitoes of Edisto Beach, South Carolina, rejoice in regularly doing major damage to her! No doubt, staying on the fourteeth floor of a Moscow apartment building saved her on a number of years—but how does one explain June and July in various locales on the Trans-Siberian train with no problems? However, the legions of those who have suffered from the mosquitoes strongly advise that travelers take from home antihistamine and repellent cream. Local products may not be effective, and foreign ones not available.

## Money

*Cash*   All travelers face decisions on how much money, and in what form, to take abroad. Dollar bills need to have been issued since 1990, in good condition, with no writing on them. It is preferable to have the newer design bank notes of $20 and larger. The U.S. Treasury introduced a new series of $100 bills in 1996 and of the $50 in 1997. Counterfeiting is a popular "sport" in the former Soviet Union and Eastern Europe, and banks are very vigilant to avoid being swindled.

Change dollars in a bank, "bank"/**банк**, or at an official exchange venue, "ob*men* va*lyu*ti"/**обмéн валю́ты**. A passport is necessary, and be certain that the bank gives a receipt (a kvi*tan*tsiya/**квитáнция**) or a certificate (a *sprav*ka/**спрáвка**). They may be needed upon leaving Russia. Exchange windows inside banks are the safest. Travelers who have changed money with people who approach them on the street and offer them a "deal" repeatedly report having been cheated. The exchange rates in banks and the exchange venues are very similar; unless one is changing a very large amount of money it is not worth seeking the absolute lowest rate. Most banks will not accept denominations lower than $20. One dollar bills may be useful for tips, but not to buy rubles.

*Credit Cards*    Hotels, restaurants, and shops that cater to foreign travelers generally accept credit cards; other do not. Of the various credit cards, Visa is most widely accepted; however, it is best to have a backup card, such as MasterCard or American Express, though the later may not be accepted outside Moscow and St. Petersburg. However, within those two cities an American Express card may be helpful in obtaining money when combined with a personal check, as described below. Credit cards with cash advance capability are very helpful in the event of a cash emergency. Before traveling abroad, it is wise to leave one's credit card account information with a family member should a traveler need to cancel a credit card if it is lost or stolen. Russian phones are rotary (pulse) dial and do not interface with U.S. companies' automated services. Likewise, 800 numbers may be difficult to use; moreover, they are not free from Russia. (See Point 65, "Telephone.")

*Travelers' Checks*    Travelers' checks are the safest way of bringing money abroad. However, they are difficult to cash or use as payment for services in Russia, especially outside of St. Petersburg and Moscow. The Metropol, a luxury hotel in Moscow, does not accept them in payment. The banks that do cash them, and also the American Express offices in St. Petersburg and Moscow, charge about 3 percent to cash each individual check. Both Visa and American Express checks are accepted; however, the latter are easier to replace if lost or stolen (but only in person and only in St. Petersburg and in Moscow).

An advantage American Express cardholders have is that they can obtain cash advances in American Express's St. Petersburg and Moscow Offices with a personal check. However, this does not apply to *Optima* American Express Cards.

*ATMs*   Automated teller machines exist in various points in larger cities. However, because of ATM fraud, as of the early 2000s, ATMs are not considered safe by international standards—not to mention the unsavory charcaters who may be lurking nearby. Middlebury University's School in Russia participants are advised not to use them but to rely instead on bank teller windows. Foreign visitors who want to obtain cash advances with their ATM cards should make certain that a credit card logo also appears on them. The money will be received in rubles, although travelers have indicated that there are some rare ATMs at which it is possible to receive dollars.

*Western Union*   One can have money wired to many Russian cities. To do so is fairly expensive, however, because there may be a $65 fee for sending $1,000. Typically money is received in rubles, although some Western banks may pay in dollars, at an extra charge. It generally takes from two to five days for such a transaction.

*Security*   When in Russia's major cities, foreign visitors should be as careful as in any other major city in the world. The criminal activity of Russia that is recorded in the U.S. media is generally of the kind that originates from the Russian Mafia and is aimed at citizens of Russia, be they very rich businessmen, journalists, or politicians. Tourists, by and large, do not fit into this category. However, foreign visitors need to be aware of pickpockets as well as of Gypsies, who swarm, overpower, and steal. As mentioned elsewhere, it is important that care be exercised when exiting Money Exchange points and after using ATMs. It is best to blend in as much as possible with Russians. Items and behavior that identify a person as a foreign visitor are loud, colorful clothing; fanny packs; baseball caps; and walking down a city street with a long, arm-swinging stride while smiling. (Russians reserve their smiles for family and friends.)

For safety reasons, travelers in Russia, especially those who do not speak Russian, should use only official taxis. A green light on the window or roof is an indication that a taxi is looking for passengers. One should not get into a taxi if it is already carrying another passenger. When hailing a taxi, it is quite possible that a private car owner, "*chast-nik*"/**частник**, will stop and offer a ride; it is a way for Russians who own cars to earn extra money. Although convenient, catching a ride this way can be dangerous and should not be undertaken by persons traveling alone. Foreigners have been known to have been robbed under such circumstances. When using a "chastnik," after indicating your destination, it is wise to agree on a price at the outset.

## Health Considerations/Medical Care

Travelers in Russia should take normal precautions similar to those taken in many other countries: avoid drinking tap water, boil or peel all vegetables and fruits, and do not purchase food sold at street kiosks.

In its Consular Sheet on Russia (available at http://travel.state.gov/Russia.html), the U.S. State Department states the following:

*Medical Facilities:* Medical care is usually far below Western standards, with severe shortages of basic medical supplies. Access to the few quality facilities that exist in major cities usually requires cash payment at Western rates upon admission. The U.S. Embassy and Consulates maintain lists of such facilities and English-speaking doctors. Many resident Americans travel to the West for virtually all their medical needs; such travel can be very expensive if undertaken under emergency conditions.

*Medical Insurance:* U.S. medical insurance is not always valid outside the United States. U.S. Medicare and Medicaid programs do not provide payment for medical services outside the United States. Doctors and hospitals often expect immediate cash payment for health services. Uninsured travelers who require medical care overseas may face extreme difficulties.

Check with your own insurance company to confirm whether your policy applies overseas, including provision for medical evacuation, and for adequacy of coverage. Serious medical problems requiring hospitalization and/or medical evacuation to the United States can cost tens of thousands of dollars. Ascertain whether payment will be made to the overseas hospital or doctor or whether you will be reimbursed later for expenses you incur. Some insurance policies also include coverage for psychiatric treatment and for disposition of remains in the event of death.

✻

# 71. TRANSPORT, TRAFFIC, ACCIDENTS, AND HOW TO COPE WITH A MILITIAMAN (POLICEMAN)

The major Russian cities, which until the late 1980s were relatively free of traffic jams, have begun to experience road congestion. The number of cars on Moscow's streets increased tenfold in the 1990s. The rush hours, chas*i* pik"/**часы́ пик**, are from 7:00 to 9:00 in the morning, and from 4:00 to 7:00 in the evening. During this time, metro cars, buses, trolleys, and the streets of the cities are very crowded. Weekends bring no relief, because a large part of the population heads for dachas in the countryside.

Russia has been justifiably proud of its transportation system, with the metro systems in Moscow and St. Petersburg, and with bus, trolley, and streetcar networks in other cities. However, as more people have moved into cities while the number of buses has been reduced to save energy, the transportation system has become overloaded. Russians complain that, with fewer buses on the streets, it is taking them longer and longer to get to work.

Visitors should be aware that many Russian drivers drive as if they, not the pedestrian, have the right of way on Russian streets. It is always wise to look in all directions before crossing a street. At many street intersections in big cities, underground passageways, "pere*kho*di"/**перехо́ды**, have been constructed. Crossing the street without using them may lead to a "shtraf," fine (**штраф**).

An unusual feature of driving in Russian cities is the U-turn permitted, when indicated by the appropriate street sign, in the middle of a street.

Traffic accidents are a common sight in Russia. First of all, traffic laws are often ignored. Moreover, even though there are frequent checks by the militia, drunk drivers abound, and the result is many accidents.

"*Sk*oraya *po*moshch," the ambulance service (**Ско́рая по́мощь**), used to have, by and large, an excellent reputation. The ambulances arrived quickly and were staffed by skilled doctors. By early 1994, however, the quality of this service had declined. The ambulances, a "Rafik" brand van produced in Latvia, were in need of repair, but parts were unavailable because Latvia required payment in hard currency.

There are two types of militia, as Russian policemen are called. "Militsio*ner*i"/**милиционе́ры** are in charge of maintaining order on the streets and in public places where people gather. Another group, formerly called "Ga*ish*niki"/**ГАЙшники** (but for whom there is no term as of yet), are in charge of Traffic. They see that road laws are obeyed, set up roadblocks to check on the sobriety and legality of drivers, stop motorists for speeding, and check on weight limits of trucks. When a traffic policeman stops a Russian driver, what happens next depends on the personalities involved. Many Russian drivers carry emergency gifts for the policeman in order to favorably influence him. If a policeman is interested in a "gift," he is likely to invite the offender to his car, so that the gift can be offered in private.

❁

# 72. TSERETELI, ZURAB KONSTANTINOVICH

*Zurab* Konstan*tin*ovich Tsere*teli*/**Зура́б Константи́нович Церете́ли**, controversial sculptor, painter, architect, and maker of mosaic murals, was born in the Soviet republic of Georgia in 1934 and studied at the Tbilisi Academy of Arts. Early in his career he was awarded a Lenin Prize for a design of a children's village in Adler by the Black Sea. He was chosen to be the chief architect/interior designer for the Moscow 1980 Olympics. Since then he has been headquartered in Moscow and is strongly supported by mayor Yury Luzhkov. His sculptures can be found in London, Paris, Rio de Janeiro, and Tokyo, among other cities. In New York his 39-foot-tall, 40-ton composition sculpture of St. George slaying the dragon, "Virtue Conquers Evil" ("*Do*bro pobezh*da*et zlo"/**Добро́ побежда́ет зло**), stands in front of the United Nations headquarters, a gift of the Soviet Union on the United Nations' 45th anniversary. It was constructed from actual parts of Soviet and American dismantled nuclear missles. To commemorate the 500th anniversary of the discovery of America, Tsereteli sculpted a 160-foot representation of Christopher Columbus; after difficulty in finding a home for it, the sculpture was finally installed in Seville, Spain, to acknowledge the fact that Spain is the country from which Columbus set sail.

In Russia, Tsereteli plays a leading role in the Academy of Arts (he has been president of it) and has received many awards for his works. The majority of them are to be found in Moscow, including the sculpture group "Tragedy of People" in Victory Park and the outside decorations on Christ the Savior Cathedral. Controversy surrounded his reconstruction of the Manezh Square in the very center of Moscow and the sculpture animal group in Aleksandrovsky garden between the Square and the Kremlin walls. Even more controversial is the monument, about 150 feet tall, to Peter the Great, located on an isthmus of the Moscow River. It was constructed to commemorate the 300-year anniversary of the founding of the Russian navy by Peter the Great. Peter the Great is standing on a sailing ship, looking forward. The work is criticized for its pretentiousness and for failing to adhere to scale—the figure of Peter the Great is much larger proportionately than the ship on which he stands. Tsereteli's defenders, however, point out that the symbolism of Peter the Great, as the Russian leader who "opened the window" to Europe and who founded the Russian navy, is evoked by the sculpture. No doubt the ambivalent attitude of Russians towards Peter the Great as a historical figure influemces how they view the sculpture.

When Tsereteli rejected the demand of some Georgians not to invite President George H. Bush to his Moscow studio, his sculpture "Rings of Friendship" in Tbilisi was blown up and his studio there burned. Possibly to avoid a similar fate to the Peter the Great monument in Moscow, the public is not allowed near it. Indeed, some bombs have been found near the monument, but detractors suggest that Tsereteli himself is responsible for the bombs, designed to draw attention to himself and his work. Nevertheless, Tsereteli is admired for his talent in fashioning visual shapes that reflect an energetic, picturesque style. Tsereteli is an example of the creative Russians who have chosen to stay in Russia and contribute to its artistic vitality.

# 73. *TY* AND *VY*, "YOU"—FAMILIAR AND FORMAL (ТЫ AND ВЫ)

Family members, close friends, children, and animals are addressed by the familiar "*ty*," you, or thou (**ты**). (Compare to the French **tu** and the Spanish **tú**.) Other people, and more than one person, are addressed by "*vy*," you (**вы**). The "*vy*"/**вы** form, together with the first name and patronymic, is the preferred form of address among Russians, even among colleagues who have worked together for many years. In some families, children address their parents with "*vy*"/**вы**. In correspondence, "*vy*"/**вы** is capitalized when addressing one person, but not when it is directed to two or more people.

Knowing when to switch from "*vy*"/**вы** to "*ty*"/**ты** takes considerable experience, and foreign visitors should use the "*vy*"/**вы** form when in doubt. Serfs and servants were historically addressed by the familiar form. The inappropriate use of "*ty*"/**ты** is a form of insult. To go from the "*vy*"/**вы** form to "*ty*"/**ты**, two people pour a drink, link arms, drink, then kiss each other once (or three times). This ceremony is referred to as "pit na bruder*shaft*"/**пить на брудершáфт.**

The use of "*ty*" or "*vy*" influences the ending of verbs: one says "*ty* chita*esh*," you [singular or familiar] are reading (**ты читáешь**), but "*vy* chita*ete*" you [plural or polite] are reading (**вы читáете**). Even the most common way of saying "hello" is affected. "*Zdravs*tvuy"/**Здрáвствуй** is said to people with whom one is on a "*ty*" basis, but "*zdravs*tvuy*te*"/**здрáвствуйте** to people with whom "*vy*" is used.

# 74. VACATIONS

The length of vacations varies. Most Russians generally have 24 working days (i.e., a month) of vacation per year. Clerical staff in schools, factories, etc., receive from 12 to 18 working days. Teachers, irrespective of where they work, receive 48 working days. People working in difficult or dangerous conditions, such as in Russia's far north, may receive additional vacation days. By agreeing to work overtime on weekends and holidays, Russians may increase the number of their vacation days. Prior to the late 1980s, an ideal vacation for a Russian was a "put*yov*ka"/**путёвка**, a "subsidized vacation package deal," which included room and board at a house of rest or a sanatorium. Unlike the English meaning, these sanatoriums are not medical establishments, although doctors and nurses may be on the premises and, especially in the latter case, specific medical problems can be addressed. The scarcity of hotels and the poor roads make the "family driving vacations," so common in the Western world, risky in Russia. Students and other adventurous souls frequently travel and camp along the way.

After the late 1980s and into the 1990s, as republics seceded from the Soviet Union, Russians frequently were not welcome in many places that had been popular (e.g., the Black Sea and Baltic Sea resorts and the Caucasus), and the choices for vacation spots decreased. However, the vastness of Russia (the largest country in the world) offers the residents many choices. Moreover, the lessening of restrictions and the growing economy now make foreign travel possible for more Russians. By staying at inexpensive hotels, economizing on meals and avoiding expensive theater performances, Russians—and not just the wealthy ones—are able to travel abroad. (The newly rich Russians do not need to economize, of course.) Popular spots are Turkey, Cyprus, the United Arab Emirates, Europe, and the United States. U.S. Ambassador to Russia James Collins pointed out in 2000 that, whereas in prior years the American consulate issued 4500 visas a year to Russians, the number had risen to 100,000 that year.

Although many couples vacation together, it is not unusual for husbands and wives to take their vacations separately. In addition, many Russians choose to spend their vacation at their dachas.

Foreign visitors traveling to Russia on business should be aware that upon arriving in Russia they may commonly be told that key personnel are on vacation, even if the visit has been planned for several months. While on vacation, even Russian professionals normally do not contact their place of work. This practice can be worse than annoying for foreign visitors in Russia on business.

❀

## 75. VODKA AND DRINKING

Vodka, the most popular drink in Russia, is made from potatoes, wheat, or rye. In restaurants vodka (as well as other popular drinks such as cognac and wine) is sold by the gram—100 grams, 200 grams, etc. A small decanter is 500 grams. Vodka bottles sold for local consumption do not have a reclosable bottle top. This leads to many jokes about the fact that once a bottle has been opened, it needs to be emptied, frequently leading to a hangover. To get over the hangover, one needs to have a drink and therefore opens another bottle—which cannot be closed, so again it needs to be emptied, and the cycle recommences.

Through the centuries, Russians have been singled out for their heavy drinking. Almost all accounts of Russia comment on drunkenness, frequently of a "binge" nature. It has been suggested that the penchant for this type of drinking has its origins in the practice of wrapping Russian children in tight swaddling clothes, from which they were released on occasion for a wild romp. Drinking vodka, cognac, or moonshine to excess is called the "*zelyo*niy zmey," green serpent (**зелёный змей**), while the practice of drinking constantly is referred to as "podda*vat*"/**поддавáть**. To gesture that someone is inebriated or wants to drink, Russians rub two fingers together under their chins, or by the side of one of their ears.

Do not expect to be served cocktails when visiting a Russian home, nor after-dinner drinks. On the table there may be bottles of champagne, wine, vodka, or cognac. Vodka and cognac are drunk "neat" from a shot glass, immediately followed by a bit of pickle, rye bread, sausage, or herring. This practice is repeated again and again. Foreign visitors not used to such drinking need to be wary, lest they end up under the table. Pleading doctor's orders or religious convictions may be in order even if untrue. However, for credibility this needs to be declared at the beginning of a meal or event—not after one has already imbibed.

Although a guest may successfully beg off from drinking, the offering of a toast "tost" (**тост**) is nearly obligatory. Russians highly value the ability to offer toasts. Generally the first toast is made by the host or hostess or an honored guest. It is not unusual for the toasts to continue unabated throughout the course of a meal. Toasts range from good wishes regarding health ("za *va*she zdoro*ve*"/**за ва́ше здоро́ве**) to compliments to the host and hostess, comments on the magnificence of the feast, good wishes for their own and their children's future, and so on.

A visitor should be cautious when offered "samo*gon*"/**самого́н** or moonshine (generally vodka-based), and know the source well, as poisonings from samogon have not been infrequent.

## 76. WEIGHTS AND MEASURES

The metric system is used in Russia.

| | | |
|---|---|---|
| **миллиме́тр** | milli*metr* | millimeter (.0394 inch) |
| **сантиме́тр** | santi*metr* | centimeter (.3937 inch—less than half an inch) |
| **метр** | metr | meter (39.37 inches—about one yard and 3 inches) |
| **киломе́тр** | kilo*metr* | kilometer (.6124 of a mile—about 5/8 of a mile) |
| **литр** | litr | liter (1.0567 quarts—a fraction over a liquid quart) |
| **грамм** | gramm | gram (0.353 ounce) |
| **килогра́мм** | kilo*gramm* | kilogram (35.27 ounces—about 2.2 pounds) |

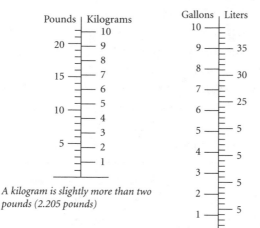

| Pounds | Kilograms |
|---|---|
| | 10 |
| 20 | 9 |
| | 8 |
| 15 | 7 |
| | 6 |
| 10 | 5 |
| | 4 |
| | 3 |
| 5 | 2 |
| | 1 |

*A kilogram is slightly more than two pounds (2.205 pounds)*

| Gallons | Liters |
|---|---|
| 10 | |
| 9 | 35 |
| 8 | 30 |
| 7 | |
| 6 | 25 |
| 5 | 5 |
| 4 | 5 |
| 3 | |
| 2 | 5 |
| 1 | 5 |

*A liter is a little more than $\frac{1}{4}$ of a gallon, that is, a little more than a quart*

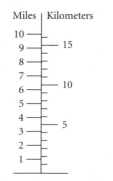

| Miles | Kilometers |
|---|---|
| 10 | |
| 9 | 15 |
| 8 | |
| 7 | |
| 6 | 10 |
| 5 | |
| 4 | |
| 3 | 5 |
| 2 | |
| 1 | |

*A kilometer is approximately $\frac{5}{8}$ of a mile.*

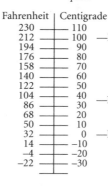

| Fahrenheit | Centigrade | |
|---|---|---|
| 230 | 110 | |
| 212 | 100 | —Boiling point of water |
| 194 | 90 | |
| 176 | 80 | |
| 158 | 70 | |
| 140 | 60 | |
| 122 | 50 | |
| 104 | 40 | —Normal body temperature |
| 86 | 30 | |
| 68 | 20 | |
| 50 | 10 | |
| 32 | 0 | —Freezing point of water |
| 14 | −10 | |
| −4 | −20 | |
| −22 | −30 | |

## 77. WORK AND PROFESSIONS

The Russian workday generally starts at 9:00 or 9:30 AM, or frequently at 10:00 AM. Factory workers, however, may start as early as 7:30 or 8:00 AM. An hour-long lunch (frequently dinner, the main meal of the day) is taken around 1:00 PM, and a tea break at 3:30 or 4:00. Work stops around 5:00 or 6:00 PM. As in most cultures there is wide variety in the Russian work ethic. Many Russians are hardworking and conscientious and take great pride in the timeliness and quality of their work. Some remember the times during the Stalin years when showing up at work even a few minutes late resulted in being arrested. During the years of central economic planning, the end of an economic plan at the end of a month resulted in deadlines that had to be kept and plans to be fulfilled at all costs. Nevertheless, the many years of government policy of low salaries, employment for all of its citizens, and extremely rare firings has resulted in a lax work ethic. The saying "The government pretends to pay us and we pretend to work," often still seems to be in effect.

The changes in Russian society since 1991 make it difficult to gauge public attitude toward the most popular or respected professions in Russia. Prior to 1991 the most respected professions in Russia were party and trade union bosses, diplomats, dentists, journalists, and radio and television broadcasters. Popular also were auto mechanics and all jobs having to do with hard currency or foreign-trade companies. Catering to the intelligentsia (see Point 34, "The Intelligentsia") ensured that the professions of artists, writers, and scientists were valued and included perks, such as free vacation passes or "pu*tyov*ki"/**путёвки** (see Point 74, "Vacations"). Since 1991, these professions have lost both their prestige and their perks. Increasingly important, though not necessarily respected, in contemporary Russia is the businessman, the entrepreneur, the owner of a venture. The generation of Russians who have grown up believing that making a profit is immoral resent the success of people engaged in such activities. "They do not create anything themselves, only charge us more for what someone else has already produced" is a common complaint by those critical of the new ways. Not only criticized but also frequently feared are the newly rich Russians, *no*vie *rus*skie/**но́вые ру́сские**—people who very quickly, and sometimes by undisclosed and frequently questionable means, became rich. About 2 percent of the population, they are usually of a low cultural level.

The fields of medicine and engineering, highly respected in the West, are somewhat less so in Russia. Except for highly specialized surgeons who are respected and receive relatively large salaries, doctors tend to be female and are paid no more than schoolteachers, another largely female, low-paying profession. For engineers, the situation is a bit more complicated. To qualify as an engineer, one needs to be a graduate of a technical engineering institute. Competition for admission to these institutes is strong, and the jobs the graduates received within the former Soviet Union were impressive. Yet, when some of these graduates emigrated to the West, some of them were told that they were not "engineers" by Western standards.

The role of women is changing in Russia in the 1990s. During the Soviet period, women were officially treated as equals with men. They were provided generous maternity leave, and their jobs were held for up to three years after childbirth. They worked in typically female positions—as doctors and teachers—as well as in jobs that demanded physical strength: construction work and house painting. They were managers of factories, stores, and research labs. Much was made of their presence in the government and party, though they rarely held top, policy-making positions. In the 1990s, with the drive for a market economy, proportionately more women than men, especially women with children, have been forced to join the unemployment ranks. In UNICEF's "Women in Transition" report in September 1999, it was reported that although women face increasing discrimination in the former Soviet Union and Eastern Europe, there have been improvements such as health care and state-funded child care.

# SELECT BIBLIOGRAPHY AND ADDITIONAL READINGS

Batalden, Stephen R., and Sandra L. Batalden. *The Newly Independent States of Eurasia: Handbook of Former Soviet Republics*, second edition. Phoenix: The Oryx Press, 1997.

Bogdanova, K., compiler and editor. *Ten Russian Poets*. Moscow: Progress Publishers, 1979, p. 242.

Bogert, Carroll. "What's Right With Russia," *Newsweek*. June 21, 1993, p.45.

Brown, Archie, Michael Kaser and Gerald S. Smith. *The Cambridge Encyclopedia of Russia and the Former Soviet Union*, second edition. Cambridge: Cambridge University Press, 1994.

Brzezinski, Matthew. "American Media Mogul Makes News in Moscow," *The New York Times Magazine*, July 22, 2001.

Corten, Irina H. *Vocabulary of Soviet Society and Culture*. Durhan, North Carolina: Duke University Press, 1992.

Edwards, Mike. "A Broken Empire," *National Geographic*. Volume 183, No. 3 (March 1993), pp. 4–53.

*The Europa World Yearbook*. London: Europa Publications Limited, 1998.

Gerhart, Genevra. *The Russian's World: Life and Language*. New York: Harcourt Brace Jovanovich, Inc. 1974; second edition, Holt, Rinehart and Winston, Harcourt Brace College Publishers, Fort Worth, 1995.

Hingley, Ronald. *Russian Writers and Society, 1825–1904*. New York: McGraw-Hill Book Company, 1967.

Hosking, Geoffrey, and Robert Service, editors. *Reinterpreting Russia*. London: Arnold, 1999.

Lally, Kathy. "Where Forbidden is a Possibility," *Baltimore Sun*, July 11, 1999.

Lewis, J. Patrick. "Russia's Rough Road," *The Columbus Dispatch*, September 19, 1999.

McDowell, Bart. *Journey Across Russia: The Soviet Union Today*. Washington, D.C.: National Geographic Society, 1977.

Morris, George W., Mark N. Vyatyutnev, and Lilia L. Vokhmina. *Russian Face to Face, Level 1*, Lincolnwood, Illinois: National Textbook Company and Moscow: Russky Yazyk Publishers, 1993.

Nadelson, Reggie. "The Letter from Moscow," *Departures*, November/December, 2000.

Putin, Vladimir, with Nataliya Genorkyan, Natalya Timakova, and Andrei Kolesnikov. *First Person: An Astonishingly Frank Self-Portrait by Russia's President*. Translated by Catherine A. Fitzpatrick. New York: Public Affairs, 2000.

Riasanovsky, Nicholas V. *A History of Russia*, fourth edition. New York: Oxford University Press, 1984.

Rice, Christopher, and Melanie Rice, main contributors. *Moscow*. New York: DK Publishing, Inc., 1998.

Richardson, Dan. *The Rough Guide—Moscow*. London: Rough Guides, 1998.

Richmond, Yale. *From Nyet to Da: Understanding the Russians*, revised and updated edition. Yarmouth, Maine: Intercultural Press, 1996.

Smith, Hedrick. *The Russians*. New York: Ballantine Books, 1976.

Smith, Hedrick. *The New Russians*. New York: Random House, 1990.

Starr, S. Frederick. "The Waning of the Russian Intelligentsia." *Newsletter of the American Association for the Advancement of Slavic Studies*. Vol. 32, No. 2 (March, 1992), pp. 1–2.

Terras, Victor, editor. *A Handbook of Russian Literature*. New Haven: Yale University Press, 1985.

Utechin, S. V. *A Concise Encyclopedia of Russia*. New York: E. P. Dutton & Co., Inc., 1964.

Vishnevskaya, Galina. *Galina, A Russian Story*. Translated by Guy Daniels. New York: Harcourt Brace, 1985.

Yergin, Daniel and Thane Gustafson. *Russia 2010 and What It Means for the World*. New York: Random House, 1993.

Zickel, Raymond E., editor. *Soviet Union: A Country Study*, second edition. Federal Research Division, Library of Congress, 1991. Headquarters, Department of the Army, DA Pan 550-95.

"Big IMF Clients Rank High on List of Corrupt," *Baltimore Sun*, September 23, 1998.

# SELECT WEB SITES

The Web has seemingly unlimited quantities of information on Russia, both in Russian and in English.

On http://www.moscowtimes.ru, the web site of *The Moscow Times*, Moscow's leading English-language newspaper, you'll find the following listings: Front Page; Current Issue; News; Business; Stock Market; Internet; Opinion; Sports; The Beat; Weekend; Travel Guide; Archive Search; PDF Edition; Jobs; Classifieds; Subscribe; E-mail Sign-Up; Advertising; About Us.

In the "Travel Guide" one sees Home; Essential Facts; Getting to Russia; While You're Here; and Contact Us. The "Essential Facts" include items for Foreign Embassies in Moscow; Russian Embassies Abroad; Health; Holidays; Internet; Language; Mail; Measurements; Media; Money; Telephones; Time; Visas; and Weather. "Getting to Russia" contains information on Arriving—Moscow, By Plane, By Train; Arriving—St. Pete (i.e., St. Petersburg); Airlines; Train Tickets; and Other Transport. "While You're Here" lists Accommodation; Getting Around, Russia, Moscow, St. Petersburg; What to See; Study in Russia; Maps; Bookstore (*The Russian Way* is advertised in it!), Bookstore; and Travel Agencies.

## News Web Sites

The following additional web sites provide news on Russia (in English, unless indicated otherwise):

- http://www.russiajournal.com—*Russia Journal*, Russia's No. 1 English-language business weekly

- http://www.rferl.org—general news from Radio Free Europe, appearing five times a week
- http://www.gazeta.ru—daily and hourly upgrades of news, in Russian (English versions on http://gazeta.ru/intnews.shtml and http://www. gazeta.ru/English.shtml)
- http://www.lenta.ru—daily and hourly upgrades of news, in Russian (English version also available)
- http://www.strana.ru—news published in Russian
- http://www.smi.ru—coverage, in Russian, of the Russian media with links to every important news outlet, including radio and television

## Government Web Sites

- http://travel.state.gov/russia.html and Consulmo@state.gov—U.S. State Department's web sites, good for information on general conditions in Russia
- http://www.russianembassy.org—The Russian Embassy to the United States site, containing useful consular information and general background on U.S.-Russian relations

## General Information Web Sites

- http://www.cdc.gov—Centers for Disease Control and Prevention's hotline for international travelers, providing information on vaccinations and other health precautions (the words "health" and "Russia" brought a choice of 550 articles!)
- http://www.infinity.ru *or* www.iro.ru—site of Infinity Travel in Moscow, a travel agency and reliable source for invitations for tourist visas to Russia
- http://www.friends-partners.org—a good site related to Russia, Russian, and Russian studies
- http://www.expat.ru—information on all aspects of life in Moscow; their front page states: "A free virtual community for English-speaking expats and Russians. Find information on life in

Moscow, topics of interest, make new friends, look for a job or housing, post a personal ad, and much more!"

- http://www.moscow-guide.ru—official city guide to Moscow
- http://www.cityguide.spb.ru—official city guide to St. Petersburg
- http://www.interknowledge.com/Russia/rushis01.htm—information on a variety of topics, such as history of Russia, transportation, art and architecture, activities, travel tips
- http://www.rispubs.com *and* http://www.russian-life.com—*Russian Life*, a well-known magazine intended to further non-Russians' understanding of Russian culture
- http://www.gorussia.about.com/travel/gorussia/—"Eastern Europe and Russia for Visitors" has answers for common questions, a section on "How To Use Public Transportation," and, under "Russian Culture/History," a listing of Russian holidays and how they are celebrated
- http://www.exile.ru—computer version of the newspaper *The Exile;* an excellent English-language resource for up-to-date information on entertainment listings and restaurants, bars, and cafes in Moscow
- http: //www.afisha.net—electronic version of the biweekly publication, featuring entertainment listings for Moscow in Russian
- http://www.museum.ru—information, in Russian, on museums in Moscow and other cities in Russia
- http://www.bolshoi.ru—home page of Moscow's Bolshoi Theater, in English and Russian
- http://www.theater.dux.ru—St. Petersburg's theaters and monthly schedule of events, reviews, etc., in Russian
- http:// www. hermitage.ru—home page of St. Petersburg's famous Hermitage Museum, in English and in Russian
- http://www.russiantvguide.com—Russian TV guide, in Russian; by clicking on "programmy" or adding /framesets/russiantvguide.htm to the home page address, television viewers in North America are provided biweekly schedules of the major Russian TV stations that can be seen here with the aid of a dish and the payment of a fee
- http://www.rambler.ru—Russian search engine on which one can find almost anything: today's TV program on ORT in Russia; the

temperature in Irkutsk; stores where one can find the latest CDs; a horoscope

- http://www.start.ru—a valuable resource that contains links to hundreds of web sites offering access to items such as a Russian cookbook, classified ads with 16,884 job descriptions, and a Moscow Business Telephone Guide (most entries are in Russian, but there is an English version of the telephone guide, including maps)
- http://www.km.ru—web site of software publisher Kirill i Mefodiy, which started out by doing CD-ROM encyclopedias in Russian on which this useful site is based

## Useful U.S. Web Site

- www.websher.net—a rich source, the "List of Lists," with access to 12 search engines, where one can find anything, from maps of Russian subways, railways, and trams to translations of Russian literature

## U.S. Professional Organizations and Institutions

- http://www.actr.org—ACTR, The American Councils for International Education, a not-for-profit education, training, and consulting organization offering programs including academic exchange, professional training, institution building, research, curricular assistance, and consulting; links to additional informative and educational sites, such as RussNet (http://www.RussNet.org), a Russian-language distance learning site
- http://clover.slavic.pitt.edu/~aatseel—web site of the American Association of Teachers of Slavic and East European Languages (AATSEEL), the oldest professional organization for Russianists; contains good links to other sites with a connection to Russia and Russian as well as to other regional ethnic communities
- http://www.fas.harvard.edu/~aaass—the American Association for the Advancement of Slavic Studies (AAASS), which fosters an understanding of Russia; the other states of the former Soviet

Union, and Eastern and Central Europe; their peoples, history, languages, and culture; as well as the transitional economics and politics of their countries

- http://www.irex.org—International Research and Exchanges Board (IREX), a nonprofit international organization that administers programs between the United States and the countries of Eastern Europe, the New Independent States, Asia, and the Near East

- http://wwics.si.edu/kennan/index.htm—the Kennan Institute of Advanced Russian Studies, Washington DC, founded in 1974, which organizes seminars featuring prominent scholars and policymakers from America, Russia and the other successor states to the Soviet Union with experience in shaping U.S.-Russian policy, and holds noon discussions on Mondays during the academic year

# INDEX